How to Make
Your Own Free Website

And Your Free Blog Too

Jason Matthews

Pismo Beach, California. USA

ISBN: 1456329731
EAN-13: 9781456329730

Subjects include: Wordpress, Blogger, Webs, Yola, web design, free website, free website builder, blogging, create a website, how to blog, SEO, Google, e-commerce, online business and more.

Also by Jason Matthews

The Little Universe - a novel

Jim's Life - the sequel novel

Better You, Better Me - for a happy life

How to Make, Market and Sell Ebooks All for Free

Get On Google Front Page

This book is dedicated to everyone
who wants a website and blog
while saving money along the way.

Table of Contents:

Introduction

Would you like your own website? For most people, the answer is yes. After all, the possibilities are endless. You may have ideas for using a website to sell products or promote something. Maybe you want one for fun or to blog about life and the world in general. In my opinion, everyone should have a website and/or a blog. The reason is because websites and blogs *connect you with the rest of the world,* and that's a powerful thing. They give you an outlet for expressing yourself in text, photos, audio and video, plus you can link the website to everything you want. These days we're becoming a global village. Social media sites like Facebook and YouTube are examples of that. Having your own website and blog adds tremendously to your internet presence in the global village.

Several years ago I didn't know how easy it was to make my own website or that it could be done for free. I was still an internet novice, a newbie, and just didn't realize how simple and affordable it could be. As a result it seemed the only way to accomplish anything online for my business ideas was to hire someone else to do the work for me. So I paid professional designers to create webpages promoting my businesses, which quickly became frustrating and expensive. I spent thousands of dollars on four different professionals to build four different sites: three websites and one blog. In each case they did their best to interpret my concepts and come up with sites that matched. Unfortunately, their work did little to advance my career.

They also charged between $45 and $120 per hour. Not cheap. No wonder it ate up my savings. Then there were lengthy delays for any updates. Whenever I wanted anything done it typically took a week to accomplish.

Finally the discovery came; *I could have built these things for free by myself.* It wasn't rocket science. I could have created the site, updated it, made changes whenever, and everything could have been done for free.

Several years ago this was an alien concept to me. Fortunately those days are over. Now if I have an idea that requires an online presence, I make the website or blog myself. It's actually easy and entirely free. Both the websites and blogs come with "site-building" software so anyone can do it. The monthly hosting is also included so there literally are no costs.

The only requirement is a bit of your time, and you too can easily make your own free websites and blogs.

Plus it's fun and rewarding to see a website online that you created. It's simple to add links to social media pages like Twitter or Pinterest, and you can embed YouTube videos, links to other websites and PayPal buttons or shopping carts to sell products.

If you're anything like me, you probably have ideas for things to do online. Maybe you have items to sell or information describing your business. Maybe you want to post photos and video of friends and family. Maybe you can create a social site that puts like-minded people together. Whatever it is you want to do online, it can be accomplished for free and this book will show you how to do it and how to do it well.

Preliminary Questions and Remarks

Before getting started, think about these questions:

- Do you want a website or a blog or both, and do you understand the difference between the two?
- Will the site have multiple pages, and will some of them have special functions like a forum or contact form?
- What would be a good domain name for your site?
- Will you sell products or need PayPal buttons?
- How will you drive traffic to visit? How will you optimize SEO rankings with Google?

These are just some of the questions you're likely to come across. I'm going to discuss each of these and many other topics in this book.

The most important aspect for building websites and blogs, *for those who aren't computer experts and want to keep it simple*, is to use free hosting sites that come with "site-building" software. This is a built-in program allowing you, the designer, to easily manage a template and add the elements to webpages that you'll need to accomplish goals.

I stumbled across these things several years ago while waiting for the last professional webdesigner to build a site for me. I was goofing around online and discovered a place where anyone could create a site for free. And so I made a "mock version" of the site I was presently hiring out for. In just a few hours, it amazed me to see a perfectly functioning site of what I was trying to do. It came together easily, it cost nothing, it worked, and I did everything myself.

Just to make things clear, *I don't know advanced HTML coding* (webpage language), and no one has to learn this anymore to create a website. Yes, you could learn advanced HTML if you want but many people don't have time for that, and the good news is you don't have to. With site-building software at your fingertips, you can easily create a functional and professional website.

But before we get to all of the instruction that follows, let me mention a few things. First, the order in which you do the coming tips is not meant to be in any sequence. You can do them in several orders and still succeed. This is just my recommendation. Some of you may not need much advice on social media links, for example, and so you may want to skim those parts. I also recommend you read through this **entirely** before getting entrenched in any one area. It's not a big book but it's jam-packed with information. Reading through it once entirely will give you a clearer idea on the whole scheme of things before getting started.

Secondly, I'm going to present you with a wealth of information. For some, most of this will be new; for others there will be parts that feel like a review. All of it has to do with online methods for accomplishing goals, so those who are less familiar with the internet and their computers may at times feel overwhelmed. Not to worry, *feeling overwhelmed by this is a natural response and something I've experienced plenty of times.* For those who feel inundated by this, please think of it as a diet or exercise program. ***All you need to do is a little bit each day.*** Follow these tips, and I promise that you'll create a totally free website and/or blog that does everything you want and receives traffic from all over the world.

There are always tutorials that go into great detail on any one of these tips I'm about to share. YouTube.com is an excellent place to watch videos that explain more fully how to do these things. I will touch on them all, some in more depth than others, but if you still need extra info just go to YouTube or do an internet search with "tutorial on *the subject you're looking for.*" I do this frequently, even for the research to write this book.

Thirdly, you're going to create accounts at websites with new usernames, passwords, images, files, all kinds of things that could become a really scattered mess across your brain and computer. It will be seriously helpful to get organized from the start. Create a new folder and call it something like, "yourownfreewebsite," where you can store everything related to this process. Keep it on your desktop for easy access. Here's how to create a new folder:

- Go to your desktop and place the cursor in empty space.
- Right click your mouse and drag down to New and then Folder and choose it. It creates one.
- You can rename it by clicking the cursor over the letters. Name it "yourownfreewebsite" and use it to store all the new stuff we're going to be

creating so that you can easily access it in the future.

Finally, if any customer of this book would also like a free pdf version that might be handier on her/his computer with all the active hyperlinks, just let me know. I don't have any way of verifying who bought the book through a retailer other than if she/he left a review, so if that sounds fair just direct me to the review and receive a free pdf copy. It is wise to give it a quick read first, then leave a review and get your free pdf with all the hyperlinks. Email jason@thelittleuniverse.com with *free pdf for my review* in the subject box.

Website or Blog, What's the Difference?

What's the difference between a blog and a website? Actually there's not a lot of difference, just subtle things. Blogs typically are updated with new additions while websites change less frequently. Characteristics that set most blogs apart from websites are: entries are a series of posts, they're arranged by date of entry, they usually have comment boxes for visitors, often an RSS feed (Really Simple Syndication) or subscription link, previous posts are categorized by month and archived, and they often don't have an email account associated with them.

Blogs don't have to be updated regularly; they're just designed that way. They can have totally static pages and can function very much like a website. Both blogs and websites are extremely important, and both can be acquired and easily designed for free.

A lot of people have no idea how important a blog can be to their online platform. You can think of your blog as your home base, the one area that leads to everything else online about you. At the blog site you can have as much information about you as you want, plus it can be updated regularly with new articles, photos, video, etc. Fortunately, there are free places to create a blog. Notice, for the free domain name your site will have a URL like domainname.wordpress.com or domainname.blogger.com, but it really doesn't matter. The vast majority of people click links to get to websites; they don't have to manually type or remember a URL's name. Or you can pay about $10 per year for a custom domain name, like example.com, and still have free hosting.

There are dozens of options for venues to create a free blog and/or website. There are even more hosting companies that can provide space for your sites. However, unless you know or want to learn HTML coding it will be necessary to build a website and blog that has everything provided plus an easy to use site-building program. For those who really want to make a site from scratch, I'll be talking about how to do that with a program called Kompozer in a later chapter called Other Things You Can Do. The advice for all the widgets, hyperlinks, SEO tips, shopping cart, PayPal buttons and everything else will still be handy to learn for the Kompozer people. For the rest of us, having a site-building program makes it so much easier.

That's the key which makes it possible for anyone to do this: a site-building program. If you're familiar with software like Microsoft Word, Mac Paint or Microsoft Paint programs, or even if you've designed a Facebook page, then you can easily work with a site-building program. And if you haven't used those things yet, you can do this. There are tons of online tutorials at these venues and at YouTube, and I'll be giving plenty of basics as well.

Before we begin building a website and blog, you'll have to decide on a URL domain name. It's among the first thing these companies will ask for and once you choose a URL name, that's a done deal. URL stands for Uniform Resource Locator which is fancy talk for your website's address, like http://www.example.com. Of course, you can always use a 301 permanent redirect or create an entirely new site with a different URL later if you don't like the name, but you can't change your URL as easily as you can rename a folder, file or document. It can be done, but because of the efforts involved it's best to come up with the great name from the start.

Deciding on a Domain Name

Before you run off and create any website or blog, take some quality time (as in hours or even days) to think about and research the domain name you'd like. It might be catchy while conveying some aspects of you, your book or business. It will also help dramatically with search engines if the words within the URL domain name are related to any possible internet search terms for someone looking for what you have to offer.

As an example, let's say you build and sell solar powered birdbaths with little fountains and heated water for cold winter days. (These things actually exist.) You were thinking of naming the website cutelittlebirdiebath.com. While it's an adorable name, nobody ever searches that term on Google and therefore that name won't help with people who are searching for your product. A smarter named would be solarbirdbath.com or something similar. Perhaps it's boring, but that would help a bunch if someone wanted a solar powered birdbath with a fountain and heated water, and so they went searching online by typing the phrase "solar birdbath." Hard to believe, but it's a term which gets typed into Google searches 1,900 times per month (stats from

September 2014). As for the plural of the phrase, "solar birdbaths," that only gets searched 320 times a month in comparison. Based on this data, it would be smarter to name your site solarbirdbath.com than solarbirdbaths.com. Surprisingly, the "s" at the end makes a difference with search engines, which attempt to give searchers exactly what they're seeking. However, what if you knew "solar bird bath" with the extra space was searched 6,600 per month and "heated bird bath" was searched 8,100 per month?

Homework is mandatory to discover which terms and phrases related to your website title will be searched the most and how much competition from other advertisers exists already. How did I come up with those statistics and how will you do similar research?

By using Google Keyword Planner and researching keywords in general. This advice is not just for making websites but for research before anything you post online (press release, articles, blog posts, etc.)

Keywords are essential to help search engines like Google and Bing link any webpage to certain words, terms or phrases. It's best to add keywords to every site, blog and location that has boxes for them, keywords that describe the content of what your site is about. And, as shown above, you can even figure out ways to include keywords in your domain name.

For example, let me explain how I came to decide on the title for this book and the websites. The book is entirely focused on teaching others to create free websites and blogs. During the initial brainstorming sessions, I wrote down the major keywords and phrases that came to mind. Here's the partial list:

Create free website

Build free website
Make free website
Make free site
How to build free sites
Create free blog
Make a free blog
How to make free websites
Make my own website
Make your own website
My free blog
Your free website

And so on. The next step is to go to Google Keyword Planner - http://adwords.google.com/keywordplanner (formerly known as Keyword Tool, and now you will need a free AdWords account). There you can input these phrases individually or altogether and get valuable feedback from Google on which search terms are used the most and how much competition exists from other advertisers. By comparing each of these plus the synonyms, or similar terms Google automatically provides, it becomes clear which keywords should work best over time.

Back to our example. By comparing extremely similar phrases like "create free website," to "build free website" and "make free website," Google told me that "make free website" was a more common search term than the others (back in 2010). I also learned that "website" was more commonly searched than "site" and "blog" when mixed with the rest of the phrase. Another revelation was that "your" was more commonly searched than "my" when mixed with these other phrases. I also wanted to include the word "own" because it implies ownership and only slightly reduced the number of searches per month. Making sense?

In less than an hour I had narrowed my book title and website URL down to these possibilities:

Make your own free website
How to make your own free website
Your own free website

I checked the competition from other advertisers, which is also included in the Keyword results. It turns out when comparing "make your own free website" to "your own free website," they had identical monthly searches and similar competition from other advertisers, so this left the decision up to me and I prefer to go with fewer words when possible.

Then I checked name availability at both Godaddy and the websites where I wanted to create free examples for this book. Although this domain name was not available at Godaddy as a pure dot com, it was available at the venues to create my examples. And so I registered it as yourownfreewebsite.webs.com and yourownfreewebsite.yolasite.com. (Know this; the free version will have the extra suffix, and a change to a pure dot com or other suffix is only about $10 per year. I have both versions of domain names: free and custom, but the custom domain names admittedly do better in time with search engines.)

Additionally I battled with whether to use dashes, underscores or nothing to separate the words in the URL. Should the site be called your-own-free-website, or your_own_free_website or simply yourownfreewebsite? All of the research indicated that Google would find it just fine since they have such a complex algorithm with over 200 variables for detecting keywords, so this really boils down to personal preference. In the end I liked it this way, your-own-free-website.com because I believe it's the easiest to read. Remember, you don't have to use dashes or underscores for Google to find the keywords in a URL. For that site I spent a few bucks to have the custom domain name without the extra suffix, though for demonstration purposes I also created your-own-free-website.webs.com to show others not to worry about the extra suffix.

So take your time not only brainstorming for names but also using Google Keyword Planner to research the intelligence of your options. *Ideally you can find some keywords that have low competition from other advertisers and high numbers of searches from users each month*.

http://adwords.google.com/keywordplanner

Remember to also check its availability as purely a .com, as in solarbirdbath.com, because someday you may want to spend a few bucks and make the conversion. Name availability is easy to check at many places including Godaddy - http://www.godaddy.com/. If you find the perfect name for your website and a registrar like Godaddy confirms that it is available, then you might want to spend around $10 per year to reserve that domain name even if you're not ready to install it. The reason is so it will be there when it's needed, and no one can take it from you. Even if the dot com is not available, there are also options like solarbirdbath.info, solarbirdbath.net, solarbirdbath.biz and solarbirdbath.me.

Next step, let's look at website and blogging hosts with site-building software.

The List of Free Website Companies

I'm going to make a list of website companies that offer both of these important things: free hosting and site-building tools. In the following chapter, I'll do the same thing for blogging companies. After listing them, I'll go into greater details with the ones I recommend you use. However, you may decide another company is right for your needs and that's okay. The tutorial will still *basically* be the same for any company as this is quickly turning into *universal* terms. In order for you to decide what's in your best interest, it makes sense to see what's out there before jumping into the very first one.

This is a partial list first written in September of 2010, updated regularly and most recently in September of 2014 because things change quickly in the industry. There are new companies coming out all the time and dozens that I haven't mentioned here. Please be aware of those facts, although I do believe the venues that follow are the best for most people. These sites typically require users to be at least 13 years of age, that the sites do not contain profanity or pornography and that other common decencies are followed.

(Also it should be noted all of these sites have introductory options that are totally free, while if you want to upgrade for things like more storage space, personalized domain name, more pages, no ads in some cases, email accounts, etc.—that can also be done for very reasonable prices.)

Here's the list of free website companies I recommend you try out:

Webs.com.

This was formerly called Freewebs.com and not to be confused with Web.com, which did not make my recommended list.

Webs.com is among the all-around best companies for creating free websites. I've personally created three websites through them including one of the examples for this book, http://your-own-free-website.webs.com. They have so many pros going for them such as a great site-building program, hundreds of templates to choose from, every type of widget and add-on you should ever need, a knowledge forum of support consisting of other members, customized apps and more. I've never had a major problem with them, and the few times I've had minor problems they've always been cleared up within 24 hours. From their site;

At Webs, we provide all the tools you need to create a professional-looking website in just minutes. Add a blog, forum, calendar, photo gallery, video gallery and much more. Want to turn your site into a social network? No problem! You also have the ability to add members and create personal profiles so you can turn your site into a community where friends, colleagues and family can connect and collaborate.

The free version at Webs.com currently gives you about 42MB of storage space and a bandwidth capacity of 500MB.

To put some perspective on that, everything a visitor clicks on or downloads takes from the monthly bandwidth. Pictures, files, etc., things that get clicked on all slowly deplete your monthly allotment of bandwidth resource. For starting out, this bandwidth allotment should be fine for most anyone. If you have massive amounts if video or visitors, you may want to look into an upgrade at a reasonable price or another venue, like Yola below.

Perhaps the main complaint with Webs.com free sites is the one small forced ad on the side of your webpage. This is not a pop-up but just a small ad. For me, this is not a big deal as I see ads on Facebook, YouTube, Yahoo, ESPN and just about every other world-class site I frequently visit. The ad is always chosen to be in line with the subjects of your site, making them even more tolerable. However if signing up for AdSense by Google is something you'll insist on doing, then the free Webs.com program will not work. You may have to use another service or upgrade to a Premium package for $4/month if you absolutely have to remove the forced ad and make way for something like AdSense (which is a requirement by AdSense for any web-hosting company: no additional ads on the page).

I use Webs (and Yola) for examples and therefore go into great detail for them specifically. If you research online you'll find people who love Webs.com and people who don't, but I promise you there are way more people who love them. Of course if you choose another company, that's fine too. My advice will work with any of these below.

Yola.com.

Yola is one of the best places to make free websites and they have no ads. If you do the research, you'll hear a lot of satisfied customers who built sites at Yola.com, formerly called Synthasite and based in San Francisco. I have built an example site at http://yourownfreewebsite.yolasite.com. If you visit the site you'll notice this is the one that I spent a few bucks for the custom domain name, http://your-own-free-website.com. This is what the company says about Yola;

With Yola, if you can edit a document, you can build a free website. Yola's award-winning support team is always available, making websites easy to manage and simple to change. Yola packages include over 100 ad-free customizable templates, so you can create a website you'll love without annoying pop-ups. Yola gives you the features you want, including integration with YouTube, Google Maps, and PayPal. With Yola, you'll get two free websites with 1GB of storage so you can claim your rightful place on the web. You can purchase your own custom domain name, or decide to use a subdomain that comes with the free website hosting Yola provides. Yola's award-winning support team is always available to not only walk you through the steps to make a free website, but also to provide tips and tricks for making your website stand out and give you a website you're proud of.

What a like about Yola is the lack of a forced ad (that's right, no ad for the free version) and the extra storage space. 1GB (gigabyte) of storage is a lot, especially for those who have ample amounts of video and/or audio to present. Drag and drop features make it incredibly easy for anyone to build the pages. They also have a Properties tab on each page for Keywords and SEO tools, a great support staff and forum of helpful people. Additionally, Yola is a great choice for those who want a free site including AdSense by Google for extra income potential.

Weebly.com.

Like Yola, Weebly.com also has drag and drop editing. It comes with over 70 templates, the same content components as the others, and there are no forced ads so AdSense is a possibility. It also has an easy to use SEO tab for adding custom keywords, headers and footers. Many users love Weebly, and its reviews are generally very good. From their site;

Building a website on Weebly is unlike anything you've ever experienced. Our drag & drop website builder makes it dead simple to create a powerful, professional website without any technical skills required. Over 6 million people and small businesses have joined Weebly to build their online presence.

Content elements (like text, photos, maps, and videos) are added to your website by simply dragging & dropping them into place. Text is edited just like in a word processor. Building your website is done in real time, right from within your web browser. There's absolutely nothing to install and no upgrades to worry about.

As usual with all venues, I found some complaints as well but most happy users. Check them out and see what you think.

Webstarts.com

Drag and drop features, e-commerce and SEO optimization are among the main points the venue discusses for their free sites. 5GB of monthly bandwidth is huge but 10MB of storage isn't much compared to most others. Webstarts also limits the free sites to 5 separate webpages, which could be ample for some people. This might include pages like Home, About Us, E-Store, Contact and Links for example.

Google Sites.

What I like about this outfit is that it's run by Google, the king of most things internet. What I don't like about the venue is the lack of introductory material (as of this writing) for beginners to get a sense of what it's all about. First-time visitors are merely greeted with a page that asks you to input a URL and choose a template without any tutorial video or text meant to assist the process. It's like a wham-bam-thank-you-ma'am introduction. They do offer a good size of monthly bandwidth at 100MB and are obviously designed to be used with anything on Google like AdSense. Because Google is so important for everything online, Google Sites should be considered as a valuable option for free venues. If you want more info, watch a few tutorial videos at YouTube on making Google Sites or Google Sites tutorial.

Forumotion.com

This venue is specifically designed for people who want to create forums. Even though the other venues I mentioned have pages that can be customized for forums or member's areas, what Forumotion is doing is somewhat unique. They offer unlimited forum users and messages, domain name and customized email addresses, over 3000 templates and a huge support forum to help with questions. If strictly building a forum is the main purpose for your site, then Forumotion is a great way to go.

Etsy.com.

Etsy is a community and a company of buyers and sellers. They are made up primarily of artists selling everything from sculpture to wedding accessories. From Etsy's home page;

Our mission is to enable people to make a living making things, and to reconnect makers with buyers. Our vision is to build a new economy and present a better choice.

Etsy makes it easy for anyone to set up shop and begin selling products. There's no registration fee to get started. They charge modest fees for listing an item (20 cents per item) and take a small cut of any sale (3.5% transaction fee).

Etsy is a great way to go for artists who simply want to add their products to existing sales templates. Additionally, artists who use Etsy will benefit from the tremendous amount of daily visitors that are already aware of the site. One idea for this type of person is to create an Etsy store as well as their own website or blog. Why not, especially when it's free?

Deviantart.com

This is similar to Etsy, but DeviantART is tailored to art that is more digital and less physical. DeviantART attracts painters, photographers, game makers, designers, film makers, animators, poets, writers and more. They claim over 100 million original works of art from over 19 million users and 45 million people per month visiting. You can set up a profile, create a gallery, connect with art-lovers around the world and sell your work.

Wetpaint.com

Wetpaint specializes in wiki websites. These are sites that can be edited and contributed to by everyone who visits the site like Wikipedia, the free online encyclopedia edited by anyone. This can be used for both personal and business uses, but it clearly is designed for those who want to manage a collaborative website. In a way this could be considered both a website and a blog, for it is continually evolving. Wetpaint is ad supported, extremely easy to use, and novices can get a feel for the service by adding to other people's sites before building their own. Wetpaint communities include fans of celebrities, TV shows, movies, bands, books, athletic groups, hobbies, chefs, animal lovers, technology lovers and more. One way to see what people gravitate to on Wetpaint is by checking out several of their top sites which are listed on the home page. There you'll get a sense of how it works, what others like, and maybe you'll find some great ideas to incorporate.

Some other fine choices:

Webnode – No ads, make as many sites as you want for free, very affordable upgrade to 3 GB bandwidth if wanted at just $3/month. http://www.webnode.com/

uCoz – 250 templates, custom domain name, 400MB storage, has ads but cheap upgrade to $3/month. http://www.ucoz.com/

Wix – 500 MB storage and 500 MB monthly bandwidth. Good for flash. Has Wix ads for free sites. http://www.wix.com/

Jimdo – 500 MB storage, ad supported. http://www.jimdo.com/

Remember, there are dozens of others I haven't listed and more are popping up all the time. Currently, I believe these are the best choices for the majority of people, although some may discover venues that work better for their needs. At the same time, the advice I give for one website will still work on another—you may just have to tweak the instructions a bit.

Plus there is another option. If you really want to build a free website entirely from scratch, as in without premade templates and site-building software, you can do that too. I only recommend this for people who are very computer savvy and like to challenge themselves and/or doing things their own way. For those interested, I'll explain this in more detail in the Other Things You Can Do chapter.

The List of Free Blogging Companies

Fortunately for blogging, there's not as many companies that I recommend, and the top two are unquestionably the most popular and functional. The others have certain high-points, especially for niche topics like traveling, forum-building or sharing videos. For Wordpress and Blogger I will go into great detail in the chapter on building your blog site; for the others I will touch briefly on them here, and you can decide to investigate if they better suit your needs. Keep in mind, the advice for building these sites is fairly universal so my advice will still work at a different host with just some minor alterations.

Wordpress.com.

Wordpress is a favorite and one of the biggies I recommend. It's consistently mentioned in the best free blog sites and usually it's listed as number one. (Note—there is a Wordpress.org which is like a template with a free download but you will need to host it somewhere, probably with a paid web host. Wordpress.org does have more options than Wordpress.com, but Wordpress.com is self-hosted and entirely free.)

It's an easy to use, hosted blog service that allows you to create an unlimited number of blogs (and pages) and submits your site to the Google blog directory. Wordpress is also noted for its traffic-monitoring stats and search engine rankings. It has no forced ads, spam-killing technology for comments/trackbacks and a fantastic support forum. You can use their professional page templates or customize one to fit your needs as well as load one totally from scratch. Plus they give you a whopping 3GB (3,000MB) of storage space, which is a ton compared to any other free service. What more could you want, right? With Wordpress, you can follow their tutorials to make a great blog site in little time. I recommend giving Wordpress a try if you haven't yet.

Wordpress has very few cons, primarily that they don't allow JavaScript (can be dangerous and used maliciously). Because they don't allow certain types of coding, it means some applications like PayPal buttons, are a bit trickier to implement. (I'll give a detailed tutorial on implementing PayPal buttons to Wordpress blogs later.) They also do not allow AdSense by Google so if that is mandatory to you, read below to the next venue.

http://www.wordpress.com/

http://en.wordpress.com/features/

Blogger.com.

Blogger is the other biggie I like. It has been around since 1999 and was bought by Google in 2002. It's extremely popular, user-friendly, ad-free, and since Blogger's owned by Google it's also perfect for signing up with AdSense, Google Affiliate Network and being listing in the Google directory. It added traffic monitoring stats back in July of 2010, which was a much needed addition, although the stats are still inferior to what Wordpress provides. Blogger has tons of customizable template choices plus a great tutorial area and forum. Blogger is where I started my first blog, http://www.thebigbangauthor.com (I paid a bit extra to have the domain name like it is and continue to pay $10 per year for that), and I've been extremely happy with it. Both Wordpress and Blogger are great places to create a blog. People constantly argue over which is better.

https://www.blogger.com/start

For most people, Wordpress or Blogger would be fine. The one thing I like more about Blogger is that they make it easier to use Javascript gadgets. Plus you can use AdSense from Google with Blogger, if that's important. A good idea is to Google the phrase, "Wordpress vs. Blogger" to get other viewpoints. Common opinions are that Wordpress is more professional though Blogger is easier to use and allows for extra income with AdSense. The stats are better with Wordpress. Actually, you'll find a range of pros and cons for each. A biggie for some bloggers—they don't like the fact that Google owns Blogger and can shut down your blog if they find your content objectionable while Wordpress is Open Source so blogs can be about anything and not get shut down. Ultimately, this is a personal decision so take time to research this. Or you can do what I do and make a blog on each host. Why not? It's free and you can link them to each other.

Livejournal.com.

Livejournal is another free blogging service. I haven't used it personally, but it ranks fairly high with ease of use and design tools, yet it falls short in stat monitoring and technical assistance. It's mostly preferred by site owners who enjoy adding their own CSS (Cascading Style Sheets).

http://www.livejournal.com/

As with everything on these lists, there are more options if you merely use search engines to find them. I'm just pointing out the most popular and likely the best for your needs. Here's a few more:

Blogster - catered for photos and video, also offers free image hosting. http://www.blogster.com/

Wetpaint - wiki sites, see above description. http://www.wetpaint.com/

Building Your Website

As I explained in the earlier chapter, there are dozens of options for creating a free website with a site-building program included. Even if you go with another venue than the ones I recommend, the process will basically be the same as *these terms are primarily universal.* I'm going to describe the steps to build a site at both Webs.com and Yola.com. The free version of Webs.com doesn't support AdSense by Google, so if that is mandatory for you then either read on to the description for building at Yola.com or consider upgrading to the Webs Starter package which costs about $50/year.

(Side note—to make substantial money utilizing AdSense, your site will need to host massive traffic. If that's the case, it's likely your business or service will still benefit more from the daily visitors than the AdSense ads. I don't recommend letting AdSense availability be overly important for this decision unless your primary focus is benefitting from ads on your site.)

Webs.com.

(There is also a Web.com and these are two entirely different entities.)

The first thing you'll be prompted to do when building a site with Webs.com is enter some basic information like choosing whether the site is for Business, Group/Organization or Personal use and click the Get Started button. This is mostly to let Webs.com know which types of pages you're likely to need but can easily be changed in the future.

Fill in basic information like a contact email and password which will always be used upon logging in. They'll also want to make sure you're at least 13 years of age and agree to their terms and conditions which are pretty standard. *Before you choose your Site Address or URL and Site Title, make sure you have done your homework with Google Keyword Planner as I outlined in the Deciding on a Domain Name chapter.* This will help dramatically with SEO results in the future. Then you'll select a template which can easily be changed at any time without losing work, so just pick one and work with that to begin.

There's a thorough eight-minute introductory video that explains the whole process. In fact, there are over 50 excellent video tutorials for most any topic within the Webs.com site. At this link you can see all the videos that explain so many things to do at Webs.com - http://webshowto.webs.com/apps/videos/. I will explain most of the basics briefly, but that's a great way to see in detail and follow with video for anything you want more information on. There are also example websites to look at for ideas on what others are doing and what you might be able to adopt - http://members.webs.com/explore.jsp.

After logging in you'll be directed to the Site Manager which is like a command central. From there you can Edit certain pages, upload files with the File Manager, see your Site Stats or Site Settings and so on. You can also go through the Community tab to find Support forums on every topic.

Notice that the venue will automatically give you pages with names like Home, Products, About Us, Contact Us, Links, etc. These can be used as they are or Renamed with the Settings button. They can be made either Visible or Hidden (whether they are seen in the navigation bar of the website) and they can be Deleted. They can also be Viewed and Edited. More pages can be Added or Deleted. A great tip is to move your cursor over different icons that will explain what they do.

To get started, click the Edit icon for the Home page. It will automatically start Loading the SiteBuilder. That's when you're in edit mode for the Home page. You'll be prompted to add a title within a Content box that might be a welcome message to your site and a description of what it's about. These Content boxes are where the bulk of your page information will go. You can type text, create tables, add images or video, add custom HTML boxes which I'll explain soon and do many things within the body of your webpages.

You can also click the Template tab at the top and make adjustments to your background color and/or image, your Title and Footer, your Logo and Header, or advanced users can work with Advanced CSS (Cascading Style Sheets). Changes to your Template will be the same on every page, whereas a change to the body of your Homepage will only affect that page.

It doesn't matter if you understand all of this or not to begin with. Simply try some things out and see what happens. For example, you can click on the tab for Titles and Footer, then play around with typing some text into the box and adjusting the font, size and color. See how these changes alter the look of your header on your Home page?

I've made a free example for the purposes of this book at http://your-own-free-website.webs.com. There you can see how I've chosen a template, typed in my title info and filled in content boxes, etc.

You can also Enable the Sidebar which is the area to the right of the pages of the template I've chosen. If you look at my example you'll see my social media links, books for sale and more. Enabling the Sidebar is done by clicking on the Sidebar tab at the top and then clicking on the button that says, Enable Sidebars. That's what I did before inserting my social media links, widgets and more. I'll cover all of those in the chapter on Common Custom Modules/Widgets.

Whenever you want to Edit your Sidebar, just click on that area in Edit mode and you'll be directed to a page where you can add Custom or Widget Modules. Custom Modules are ones that you'll fill in specific HTML code (like for a Facebook badge) while Widget Modules will be premade ones that the company provides, like a Survey Poll. Custom Modules make up the bulk of my Sidebar Modules, and I'll explain how to add PayPal buttons, Facebook links and most any kind of widget/gadget you might need or want.

After typing in a welcome message and text that you want on the Home page, you can click the Publish button that will immediately save and post the changes to the site. Then with a visit to the URL, you'll see what the site looks like on the web.

Don't worry if it's partial and amateurish for the time being. Not many visitors will see the site in the first days because you haven't done anything to drive traffic to it. Take some time and play around with all kinds of site functions and Publish changes to see what you like or don't like. Eventually, when the site is built and running smoothly you'll put effort into marketing it.

Typing text for page titles and content boxes is fairly straightforward. Just go through the Edit button of the page you want to work on and type the text where you like. Then click the Publish button to save those changes.

Adding a link within certain words of text for another website's URL is also easy. Just highlight a word or section of text with the cursor, then click on the Link tab to Insert a Link, and choose either Another Website, Email Address, another Page of your site, a specific Paragraph within that page, or a File from your File Manager (like an ebook). When choosing to send someone to another website, I usually choose the Open in a New Window option so that person still has my page in a tab on their browser and can easily return to my website without reloading it.

You can also insert a Photo, Video or Add Ons just by clicking those tabs in Edit mode. Photos can either be added first to your File Manager, or directly uploaded from your Computer or from a URL. If a photo has a URL (web address) you'll know by clicking on it and having it open up in its very own page. Just copy and paste that URL info if this is the way you want to upload it. I usually save photos to My Computer and then upload through that option. Once the photo is in place on the page, you can alter its size or method of text wrapping just by clicking on it and the options above. You can also give your photo a URL link to go to upon a click from a user.

Video can be added in exactly the same method, either by uploading one to the File Manager first or selecting the YouTube tab and inserting the URL of a YouTube video you want. (Note that some videos require permission while others are fine to use. You may want to check with the owner if you're not sure although most owners are fine when others show their videos.)

Also become familiar with the Custom HTML box. When you're in Edit mode click the cursor on empty space and then choose the HTML Icon on the toolbar to Insert a Custom HTML. This is simply code talk for computers to know what you want to put in that box like a widget/gadget. For example, maybe you have a PayPal button (which I'll explain in the Common Custom Modules/Widgets chapter) and an HTML code for that. Just copy and paste the HTML code in the box and Insert and then Publish. You can then View the site and see the changes.

As with all of these things, play around and see what works. Watch the tutorial videos for adding any HTML code or Custom Module or Application or read about it in a couple of chapters. (Also note that it will take one week from signing up, a probationary period, before your contact email page is active, so if you try to receive an email notification from the site it will need to wait for one week. After that, emails will be immediately delivered.)

Yola.com

Visit the site and click Get Started Now, then fill in your info. They'll ask for a Website Category and description which is their way of guessing which types of pages you'll likely need. *The description will be the title of your site so remember to do homework and follow the Google Keyword Planner instructions in the chapter on Deciding on a Domain Name.* Again, this stuff can be altered later as can the info they'll ask about you and your services. Then you'll be asked to choose from template styles which can always be changed in the future without losing data.

Based on this preliminary info, Yola will create a draft version of your site. Now you can begin adding text and a variety of elements to personalize it. As with Webs.com, probably the best place to start is by watching their tutorial videos beginning with Lesson One: Create Your Homepage.

Yola will have pre-populated your website with a layout and some widgets they think will help. Keep in mind those are just suggestions and can be changed. To begin, you may as well populate your website by clicking into the widgets already on your page to add text or other content. There is also a content sidebar located on the right-hand side of the screen. Here you'll see all the tools to add content to your site.

Links can easily be added to the text by the same method as I described with Webs.com. All of this site-building is fairly universal as you'll notice the link can go to a Page of your site, an External URL, an Email Address or to a File you've uploaded to your File Manager. Just highlight some text, an image or anything with the cursor then click the Link Icon (looks like a chain) on the toolbar and select where you want that link to go. Click OK to Insert it, then either Save or Publish to the Web.

The first time you Publish to the Web they will ask what your plans are for the domain name. You can either pay them $19.95 for a custom domain name, although I wouldn't recommend this as many name registrars like Godaddy are cheaper. If you want to pay for a custom domain name you can get registered elsewhere for about $10 or less a year, and click the option for "I already own my domain name," then follow their instructions to switch the nameservers. Or the free option is to have a domain name with yolasite.com as the suffix, as in http://example.yolasite.com.

Notice that Yola gives you both a Widgets and Properties tab on the right side of the screen. While the Widgets tab is fairly self-explanatory, the Properties tab is where you can add keywords and more to help search engines find and identify your subject matter. We'll cover this more in the SEO chapter, and the advice below is from Yola.

Search engines read text to know the topic of a page, and there are three tags that specifically alert the search engine to what a page is about: the title, description and keywords tag.

Yola provides an area to edit these tags. If you click on the Properties tab on the Sidebar to the right of your screen, you will find fields to enter unique title, description and keywords tags for each of your site's page.

*The area labeled **Window Title** is where you will put your title tag. Your title tag should include the main keyword or concept of your page, your business or website name and your location if this would be important to your visitors; it should also be under 70 characters long. Here is a basic example:*

Fine Gold Jewelry | ABC Jewel Company | My Town, Texas

*The area labeled **Description** is where you will put your description tag. Your description tag should include your main keywords for the page, or variations of your keywords, as well as the name of your company and the location, if this would be important to your visitors; it should be under 200 characters long and should entice Internet users to click. Here is a basic example:*

ABC Jewel Company provides customers in and around My Town, Texas with the finest yellow and

white gold jewelry imported directly from Italy. Stop in today!

*The area labeled **Keywords** is where you will put in the main keywords for the page. Don't stuff keywords, only list keywords that apply to the content of the page. Here is a basic example:*

fine gold jewelry, gold jewelry, white gold jewelry, ABC Jewel Company, My Town Texas, TX

You will also want to try to easily blend the keywords you utilized in your tags into the content on the page of the site. Again, don't stuff them in, blend them in casually making sure to keep the flow of your content.

There are several things I like about Yola including the SEO Properties tags, the lack of a forced ad, the abundance of bandwidth and the ease of drag and drop editing. One thing I don't like about the free Yola version is every time I make a change and publish it to the web, Yola asks me if I want to upgrade to a paid version, which is like constant selling. I wish there was a box to check for stopping that. I also don't like the limited number of premade template choices compared to Webs.com or the fact that editing within the template header is limited. Other than that, Yola is my preferred place to make free sites.

For the purposes of this book, I've created a free site with Yola at http://yourownfreewebsite.yolasite.com/ which I paid a few dollars for the custom domain name of http://your-own-free-website.com. There you'll see another example of what you can do for free. Of course it is very similar to the Webs.com example, http://your-own-free-website.webs.com, but I wanted to vary it just a bit for a different look.

One thing you'll notice immediately is the Drag and Drop method of editing compared to how Webs.com handles it. Ultimately both methods are quite simple, but the Drag and Drop is an easier way.

Yola also has excellent tutorials and forums. You can research any topic for detailed descriptions or follow along with a training video for most anything possible to do on your site. Here's the link for all these support elements - http://www.yola.com/customer-support.

Remember; even though Yola will give you prompts for SEO help, I will go into more detail for that in the chapter for SEO (Search Engine Optimization).

But first I'd like to cover building your blog site.

Building Your Blog Site

I'm going to give details for building a blog at Wordpress.com and Blogger.com because they are by far the most popular and, in my opinion, the best. However, there are many other sites; perhaps another is more suited to your needs. These things are fairly universal so my advice for these below can be followed for others.

Wordpress.com.

For another ebook and program I instruct called, *How to Make, Market and Sell Ebooks All for Free*, I've used Wordpress.com to create a totally free blog site to give an example. It's online at http://ebooksuccess4free.wordpress.com. I regularly update the home page while many of the other pages remain static.

If you're just starting out with Wordpress.com for a blog, here are some basics to get you going. *Remember to do homework and follow the Google Keyword Planner instructions in the chapter on Deciding on a Domain Name.*

- After you sign up, you'll need to Register a blog. There you enter a blog name of your choice and a blog title that should be like a headline. Click to enter and Login.

- You should be sent to a Dashboard for your page, like a command central. Near the middle of the Dashboard page is a button that says Change Theme. Click on that and browse hundreds of choices from Random, A to Z, to Popular themes. And you can always change the template later without losing your work.

- After choosing a template, get started creating a blog, even a throw-away entry that you'll toss later just to get a feel for the process. As you blog along, click Update or Visit Site to save changes and check its appearance.

- From the editing area, it's always a good idea to place your cursor over the little icons for an explanation of what they do. You'll become familiar with them and the whole process. For example, when you're typing a blog post, if the area feels too small to work in there's an icon like a computer screen that says Toggle Fullscreen Mode and gives you a larger work space.

It would take an entire book to tutor someone to use Wordpress, but fortunately there's an excellent support forum with thorough answers to almost any question. If not, you can always ask a question and get tailored advice. Also do a Wordpress tutorial search on YouTube, and you'll have dozens of instructional videos to choose from.

If you use Wordpress.com, here's the way to insert your badge widgets.

- Once you've created your home page, open the tab My Dashboard. Scroll down on the left and look for Appearance. Under that is a tab for Widgets.

- Click on that and a host of Widget options appear that you can click/drag from the center to the upper right of the page to employ them into your Sidebar. The widget called Text for Arbitrary Text or HTML is the one that you want to drag to your upper right corner to employ as a Badge on your page.

- When you've done that you can open the box for editing by clicking the down arrow. Let's use Facebook for an example—the html code you can get by following the prompts here: http://www.facebook.com/badges/. Open the Text box with the down arrow, and type in "Facebook" (or whatever you choose) into the Title area. Underneath that is where you'll paste the html text code that you get from your Facebook Badge.

- Then go above and click the Visit Site button and *presto,* you should see your Facebook Badge on your blog. Click on it to check that it works. Then do this process for Twitter, LinkedIn and any other social media badge you have. All of these widgets can be moved around by dragging from the widget page. Cool, huh? I get a real kick when I see these things in place, so hopefully you will too.

How do you create your own custom badge for something like YouTube, MySpace or anything else you want to link to? There are a few ways, but the main thing is to create a URL of the image.

- In the Dashboard, click on Media and either Library or Add New. Follow prompts to upload an image. Once you see the image in your Library, click on it to View Attachment Page and again until you see it as a URL that ends in .jpg or .png after being opened. (If done correctly, it will be the only item on your screen. Skip down a few steps to "Copy that URL address.")

- A second way is to Add a New Post on Wordpress and insert a picture by clicking next to the Upload/Insert tab the icon that says Add an Image. It will prompt you to Select Files, where you will probably get it from your computer's Desktop, Pictures or Documents.

- Once you select the image it will upload and then ask where you want it and how big you want it. You can choose any size, but I prefer medium to smaller images. (Sizes can be altered later.)

- Once you click Insert into Post, your desired image will be there. You can View your site, click on the image and notice that it creates an entire page with a URL address for that image alone.

- Copy that URL address, go back to your Dashboard, Appearances, Widgets, and drag an Image Widget to the right side and insert it. You can name it as you like, but be sure to paste the URL address of your image into the Image URL box, and then copy and paste the destination page (the URL of your MySpace profile page for this example) into the Link URL (when the image is clicked) box. You can also easily adjust the Width and Height in pixels here to any size you want.

- Click Save, Visit Site and *voila,* your newly created widget is in place and functioning properly. You may have to adjust the size through the widget control and play around with pixel width and height. (Notice I have created a Google Plus badge this way as an example at http://www.ebooksuccess4free.wordpress.com. It's just an Image widget with a link to my Google Plus profile page.)

Also when you create a blog with Wordpress, you want to verify it with the main search engines here - http://en.support.wordpress.com/webmaster-tools/. This link is for verifying your site with Google and Bing search engines (Yahoo joined Bing in search), which we'll cover again in the SEO (Search Engine Optimization) chapter. It will assist you to add metatags to your site that these search engines will eventually crawl and identify. Help with this can also be found through the Dashboard of your blog. Scroll down the left side and find a tab that says Tools. Click on it and scroll down to the Webmaster Verification Tools. There you will see the boxes that go hand in hand with the metatags you'll be asked to input by using the link above to visit the search engines. And this will help too - http://en.support.wordpress.com/search-engines/ as a tutorial for the process and answers to frequent questions.

Wordpress has very few cons, primarily that they don't allow JavaScript (can be dangerous and used maliciously).

Because they don't allow certain types of coding, it means some applications, like PayPal buttons, are a bit trickier to implement. I'll give a detailed tutorial on implementing PayPal buttons to Wordpress blogs later. For now, just get familiar with creating pages, making posts, uploading images and inserting links.

So please check out Wordpress, and if it looks good just take your time and work on creating a blog when you can. Before you know it, you'll be blogging like a champ. (Note— the home page is designed to be changed and updated regularly, while other pages are designed to be more static. You can update the other pages, just in editing style and without creating a new comment box.)

Blogger.com.

Blogger is the other biggie I like. It has been around since 1999 and was bought by Google in 2002. It's extremely popular, user-friendly, ad-free and since Blogger's owned by Google it's also perfect for signing up with AdSense, Google Affiliate Network and being listing in the Google directory. (Blogger calls widgets "Gadgets," and they work the same as on Wordpress.) Blogger also doesn't have premade PayPal buttons, but it's very easy to create and add a PayPal button as an HTML/Javascript Gadget, which we'll explain in detail in the Common Custom Modules/Widgets chapter. Blogger has tons of customizable template choices plus a great tutorial area and forum. Blogger is where I started my first blog, http://www.thebigbangauthor.com (I did pay a bit extra to have the domain name like it is), and I've been extremely happy with it. You can view my blog and get a sense for some of the things I've done. Since using Wordpress, I wouldn't choose Blogger over Wordpress, but it's a fine place to create a blog. People constantly argue over which is better.

Sign up with Blogger at https://www.blogger.com/. Click the Create A Blog link. Fill in the pertinent information and begin the journey. Then choose a template and get started.

Blogger also has an excellent support forum. Find them through the Help tab and either click on the Help Forum or the Video Tutorials. One of the best videos to watch at the onset will be the getting started video at https://www.youtube.com/user/BloggerHelp. And there's even more help for blogger at https://support.google.com/blogger/#topic=3339243.

Gadget badges work here basically the same as they do on Wordpress. The process of getting there is as follows:

- After signing in you'll need to click on the Customize or Layout tab. It will direct you to a page where you can view your Navbar, Header, Gadgets (widgets) and Footer.
- Clicking on Add a Gadget will give you the options to choose from. For badges, you'll want to click on HTML/Java Script and then follow the previous tutorial to copy and paste the html text code.

Once you've Saved it, you can View your site and *abracadabra,* your badge should be in place. As with Wordpress, there are tons of other gadgets/widgets you can play around with and decide what you like best. This is a great habit to get into; **play around with these things to see what works well** and what doesn't. You can always make changes later plus you might find some pleasant discoveries.

As in Wordpress, when you're making a new post you can view and work with it in Edit HTML mode (which is more tech savvy) or you can choose the Compose mode which is WYSIWYG (what you see is what you get). Try switching back and forth to get a feel for the differences between the two. Then click the Preview button for a quick glimpse of what your post will look like. Again, make a post just to get a feel for the process since it can always get edited or deleted later.

As I said before, these blog venues below might be better for people with specific needs, and so I'll list them again.

Livejournal.com.
Livejournal is yet another free blogging service. I haven't used it personally, but it ranks fairly high with ease of use and design tools, yet it falls short in stat monitoring and technical assistance. It's mostly preferred by site owners who enjoy adding their own CSS (Cascading Style Sheets). http://www.livejournal.com/
http://www.blogster.com/ - catered for photos and video, also offers free image hosting.

Finally on blogging, remember to add keywords, labels, categories and/or tags wherever boxes present themselves to do so. These are general terms that describe the subjects of your post to help search engines and people to find your blog. Your name can also be added to these boxes as that will help with your branding. Advice on blogging would generate an entire book itself, so please look for experts in the field who dedicate blogs teaching others how to blog more effectively. A Google search will lead you to outfits like this one - http://www.problogger.net/, and there are many more. These people have written volumes on blogging and have excellent advice to make the most of any effort. Check them out for much more on the subject.

Common Custom Modules/Widgets

A widget or gadget is basically a morsel of HTML code embedded into your website, often resulting in an image and a link to somewhere else. There are hundreds of possibilities when it comes to widgets or gadgets that may assist a website to be more functional or just more fun. A list of these might include Facebook and Twitter Badges, PayPal buttons, Contact Forms, Surveys or Polls, Games, Maps, News and Weather, Recent Visitor Data, Hit Counters, Shopping Carts, Links to other sites or pages and many more. Some widgets act as links to open other webpages while other widgets work within their little windows on your page. I'll list several that are common to many websites and some details for the HTML code insertion which can be used for practically any other widget. I'll also cover Facebook and several other sites in much more detail later in the chapter on Social Media.

(A side note for those building or considering a Wordpress Blog—I have a Wordpress blog, and there are certain widgets that are less user-friendly to install because they use JavaScript which Wordpress.com doesn't allow. In most cases, there are easy fixes to get around it and still use the widgets you want. Usually the subject has already been covered in their excellent Support section or the Support Forum or even in the Widget Forum, where you can ask most any question and either read the answers from the past or get brand new replies to help. Since I love so many features that Wordpress.com has, I don't let the slight JavaScript widget issues keep me from building a blog there. Because I consider PayPal buttons to be so important, I give a thorough description of their Wordpress.com implementation below, though for many other widgets I do not since this book could get really long if I did.)

Facebook Badges.

If you have a personal Facebook page, Fan page or a Group page then you can easily insert a Badge or widget on your site, either in the body of one page or the sidebar of every page. This link will help - http://www.facebook.com/badges/. You can use one they provide or edit to your needs. There will also be choices for which type of site the badge will go to, like for Blogger or some Other site (like Webs.com). Click on your choice and copy the code below by highlighting it and Ctrl C or right click copy. Then go to your website in Edit mode and open an HTML Text box or widget and paste that HTML code there and Publish the change. That should do it. This can be done either in the body of the page or more commonly in the sidebar.

You can also create a Page Badge or Like Badge in that fashion and employ it the same way. You'll be prompted to fill in the pertinent information and then given the HTML code to add to a widget on your website. A Fan page can also be made which is similar to a Group page but subtly different. Fan pages allow users to "Like" your page with a mouse click, and they also allow certain applications.

To make a Fan page there's a link for Advertising at the very bottom of any Facebook page. Click on it and look for the link that says Facebook Page. Then you'll want the green button that says Create Page. The prompts that follow will be self-explanatory and simple to do once you're already familiar with creating a profile or group page. You can use Fan pages for the name of your business or even yourself.

Twitter Badges.

This Twitter Badge will be a clickable link from your websites for others to start following you. There are plenty, but here's a place to get a Twitter Badge - https://twitter.com/logo and there are many others like this one - http://www.twittericon.com/. Just choose a design, type your Twitter name in the box, and it will generate the code. Then copy and paste the html text code below the image you like, and when you insert it as a widget/gadget on your website or blog, it will become a cute birdie picture that people click to follow you.

Stay organized for things like this. Follow the instructions from before to make a new text document for your Facebook or Twitter Badge HTML code and save it in the "yourownfreewebsite" folder and name it "Twitter Badge HTML."

LinkedIn Badges.

The process is the same. Click Edit My Profile found in the left navigation area of the home page at LinkedIn. Click Edit Public Profile Settings in the upper right-hand corner of the Profile page. Click on the Customized Buttons link found in the Public Profile box. Choose a logo button and copy the HTML code provided next to it. This code will include a link to your public profile.

Create Custom Badges.

Surprisingly, some prominent member-style websites do not produce their own badges. For years MySpace did not have badges. However, if you want to create a custom badge that will go to your profile page on any website, MySpace for example, you can simply copy and save a MySpace logo image (found easily by Googling this term), upload it to your site and then insert a link that goes to the URL of your MySpace page. You can also insert text above or below the image that says, "Visit me at MySpace" or something like that. This can be done with any image to create a custom badge and hyperlink.

Google Plus (+1) recently added badges to their platform. More information on creating one is here - https://developers.google.com/+/web/badge/. Since it took Google so long to get this done, other places evolved making custom Google Plus badges, which are actually nicer in my opinion. A good place where you can upload your picture for the badge is here - http://turhan.me/+me/, and there are plenty more with an internet search.

It's likely you'll want badges (clickable icons) to any social media. If you're only on a few venues, the larger badges will work well. If you'd like to create an html widget for many smaller images, this is a great tutorial - http://www.digitaldeflexion.com/2012/07/adding-social-media-icons-to-blogger.html.

PayPal Buttons.

Buy Now and Donate buttons are extremely common whether you have a product for sale or want to let people know you gladly accept donations for advice and/or services. Many sites, like Webs.com, Yola.com and Blogger.com have premade PayPal widgets ready for your needs. Just click on their Widgets, Gadgets or AddOns (depending on the site) and follow the prompts to add yours. These buttons can also be made more custom at both PayPal.com or by a Google search of this term. I prefer making custom PayPal buttons for my ebooks.

- To do so, log in to your PayPal account and click on Merchant Services.
- There's a section for Create Buttons where it will give you the prompts to follow then the HTML code to cut and paste into your website.

For Wordpress blogs the process is a tiny bit trickier. Keep in mind, Wordpress doesn't like forms or Javascript so we have to use both the HTML and the Email code that PayPal provides.

- Just return to PayPal, Merchant Services, My Saved Buttons, on that same button you just made click Action and View Code.
- Select and copy both the Website HTML and the Email tab and URL address (which you'll notice is a PayPal web address) and paste these codes individually into Text documents and put them in the "yourownfreewebsite" folder.

This link will help if you want to follow with pictures - http://en.support.wordpress.com/paypal/. (The Wordpress support tutorial uses a Donate button as an example, but it works the same with a Buy Now button.)

- Now go to Wordpress and log in to your Dashboard.

- Scroll down the left and on Pages click Add New and call it "Bookstore" or something of your choosing. (If you want a choice of PayPal button images, you'll need to get another image's HTML code to display on your page. Get them here if you want - https://www.paypal.com/webapps/mpp/logo-center, and click Download to get the button's HTML code, copy it and return to the Add New Wordpress page.)

- Switch from Visual to the HTML editor and paste the button's Website HTML code into the text body.

- Switch back to Visual and you should see the button there (if not, retrace steps and try again).

- Now it's time to add the Link for the Email code into the image. Highlight the button's image, click Link and paste the Email URL code (from PayPal) into the URL Link box.

- Select it to open in a new target window if you prefer. That should do it. Preview or Publish the page and check that it's working.

You can also add a PayPal button into a Wordpress Image Widget for your Sidebar.

- Drag an Image Widget into your Sidebar and Title it, "buy *your product* for $(*your price*)." The Email code for the PayPal button will go in the lower box that says, Link URL (when the image is clicked).

- You'll have to insert a URL address of a PayPal button's image into the upper box that says, Image URL. Note that this will be an image, *something that ends in .gif or .jpeg for example.*

- Try putting that in the Image URL box and the Email code in the Link URL box. If the size isn't right just alter the Image widget's Width and Height with smaller numbers until they're good.

After purchases PayPal will notify you of sales. Respond immediately to customers to confirm shipping instructions, what to expect, how to contact you, etc.

StatCounter.

StatCounter.com is a valuable widget tool for many of my websites that don't contain built-in traffic monitoring and for those that do but don't give me all the details, like exact IP addresses. These StatCounter widgets can be invisible or visible, have many configurations and give you real-time stats of visitors.

- When you set up a widget with StatCounter, click on Add New Project. Simply fill in the blanks with the title info and URL for the page where you'll place the widget. The site should automatically give your own IP address, and it can be double-checked here - http://whatismyipaddress.com/ or by Googling another site for this.

- Then during set up for any StatCounter Project you'll want to block your own IP address from being counted by pasting it in the box for IP Blocking. This way it won't count your visits which can be a distraction if you visit your own sites regularly. This can also be done in the My Projects link; click the small wrench icon, click the Edit Settings link, paste your IP Address in the box provided (StatCounter should know your IP Address already and display it to the left) and check the box below saying you want that for all projects, click Edit Project and it's done. I also prefer to keep the results hidden or private, meaning not shown to any visitor, unless my site has so much traffic that I'm proudly displaying those results. It's your choice.

- Then you'll need to Configure and Install the HTML code by following the prompts, which works just like installing any HTML code widget into the body of a page where you want stats counted.

You can see StatCounter widgets at some of my sites including at the bottom of this blog post, http://tinyurl.com/mgjh48a. The icon will count your visit, and if you ever go to download my ebooks on the Download pages, you'll see it there too.

Map Widgets.

These are little maps that indicate where something is. This could be a business location for people who may need to drive to you, or it might be a destination like a vacation spot or country to visit. In every case, Google has lots of choices here and is tough to beat. https://developers.google.com/maps/

Recent Visitors, Live Traffic and Hit Counters.

I also like gadgets that show where recent visitors came from. I've used Feedjit, http://feedjit.com for some of mine though it doesn't appear to have the world maps version (like ClustrMaps) that I've used in the past. Now the free version only has the list of visitors which is still pretty fun. The world maps work better for websites with slower traffic since you can't see when they visited, just where they live as little dots on the globe. The list of live visitors works better for sites with at least a few dozen visitors per day.

There are also widgets like the ones at Amazing Counters - http://www.amazingcounter.com/, which are hit and web counters with hundreds of styles. It's all simple HTML code to follow the prompts, then copy and paste on your site.

A Google search for this topic will generate dozens of other venues.

Google Translate.

The internet is a global community, and many webdesigners would be wise to make their sites user-friendly for people who either don't read English or don't read it well. That's a few billion people, so not exactly a niche market. You can enable foreign language visitors to read a website by adding the translate tool and/or widget from Google. This is especially smart for websites that intend to cater to a worldwide audience. Yola makes it really easy with a drop and drag widget; other sites require a bit more implementation. Wordpress.com blogs always have walk-arounds for these things as you can discover in their forums, and I found a great one here - http://en.forums.wordpress.com/topic/translator-widget-1?replies=9#post-495741. You can see how I followed that advice and put a Google Translate link to my blog - http://ebooksuccess4free.wordpress.com/. It's a page with a tab. Notice it will also translate the websites you link to after clicking on those links, which is pretty cool too. Just remember to alter the tutorial's advice with your website's name. You can make a blank text document and copy and paste the code, then change it for your URL. This is most easily done with the Edit tab and using the Find and Replace features instead of manually changing each link, since that would take a long time. (Notice—the spacing on the pages sometimes gets altered in this translation process, and it's likely there are some errors in the translation. But hey, if it helps someone read your site who otherwise couldn't, it's probably worth it.)

Add This or Share Widgets.

If you want others to spread the word about your website and blog via email, Facebook, Twitter, Google Plus, etc., you can make it easier for them by inserting a widget designed to do that. You can find them here at AddThis.com - http://www.addthis.com/, and the insertion is the same as an HTML widget.

Other places for lots of free widgets and especially games/fun things:

The Blog Widgets, http://www.theblogwidgets.com/ - is a good place for all kinds.

Widgipedia, http://www.widgipedia.com/ - your ultimate widget resource.

Pogo, http://www.pogo.com/ – more free games.

Flash Animation Banners, Text and more.

To spice up your site with moving text or imagery, use flash animation as a lively way to draw attention to something. Flash animation covers a huge amount of widget potential for action whether it's a Mario Bros game or a moving advertisement. If you've already been to WidgetBox you've probably seen several animated games and fun things to add. I like flash for banners and text where I can promote a product or tell a story line by line. A great place for this is http://flashvortex.com/ where you can create unlimited free designs that are very impressive. Check them out and play around with different banners, texts, buttons, clocks and more. For a modest $30/year you can also upgrade to their premium features. This would make sense if you wanted to do a lot with flash advertising, and the company will honor anything you create even if the membership isn't renewed after the year is over. Your creations will still work.

SEO (Search Engine Optimization)

It's the job of search engines to find sites that match the criteria people are looking for. Ultimately it's best if search engines list your site as a place of interest for anyone using search terms related to your subjects. To begin, you'll almost surely start out deep in their results, like on page 20, but over time you'll climb ever closer to the top by adhering to the advice that follows. Back in 2008 when I finally got serious about establishing an internet presence and searched via Google for my own name, I came up on page 17 or so and felt discouraged by that. In time I slowly climbed closer to page one even though my name is common. Now my sites experience decent search results for not only my name but for my subjects of interest, which is more important to me.

Although in a funny way, you don't need to worry about the search engines finding your website. They will find it; I guarantee that. To know immediately if they've found you or not, simply type in the URL into the search box as in http://example.blogspot.com and see if it comes up at the top of the list. If it's not there, have no fear. It usually takes about a week or so before they index your site. Give it some time and try again. I'll instruct how to submit your sites directly to Google and many other search engines, but even if you don't they will still find you. How do I know? Because Google Alerts is set up to notify me on subjects like my name, my books, my download pages, etc., whenever anybody on Earth posts something on those items. It doesn't seem to matter how trivial or tiny the posting or the website is; like the concept of George Orwell's Big Brother, Google knows what's happening in Cyberworld.

However, you absolutely do want to maximize the recognition of search engines like Google and Bing *to not only find the site but to associate it with what you're trying to accomplish.* That means not only does Google see your site specializing in exotic fish, for example, but that it believes you really know everything there is to know about the exotic fish business because of the factors Google considers important. There are many ways to help in this regard, *but remember that this takes time.* Search engine indexes place value on how long a site has been in existence, and they prefer established sites with lots of incoming links, data and recorded visits over newer ones. Be patient and give it time as in months or (sometimes) even years. Many of my sites have excellent SEO factors working for them, but the fact that they're not very old still counts against me. As long as you stay diligent with the advice that follows, your sites will climb in the rankings slowly but surely. They will eventually make it to the top.

Keywords.

Keywords are essential to help search engines link you and your sites to certain words, terms or phrases. It's best to add keywords to every site, blog, URL, text and location that has boxes for them, keywords that describe the content of what your site is about. As I've mentioned several times, Google has a very helpful Keyword Planner program at this link - http://adwords.google.com/keywordplanner. There you can type in certain words or phrases and get results on how many times per month Google actually receives that exact request for information. You'll also see how much competition there is from others using those same keywords. *Ideally, you can find keywords that have low competition from other advertisers and high numbers of searches from users each month*.

As an example, let's say you sell sunglasses designed for athletes during performances. You want the business to be called something catchy like "Sport Shades." Unfortunately the phrase, "sport shades," only gets searched via Google 170 times per month, which is much less compared to "sport sunglasses" at 90,500 times per month and "sports sunglasses" at 18,100. (Note those stats are from Sept. 2014 and will fluctuate constantly.) Your business might sound more hip being called "Sport Shades," but if you really want to maximize its potential you will consider the URL being http://sport-sunglasses.com and the header of the home page containing the words "sport sunglasses" and having that phrase repeat itself once or twice throughout the text on each page of the website. Additionally, you'd benefit from having those keywords tastefully in all advertising and articles that promote the business, even if you still call the business "Sport Shades."

Have you ever seen a webpage that contained the same word repeated many dozens of times on one page? It's very unpleasant to read, but the webdesigner is trying to maximize the ability of search engines to find it. This approach is not recommended as most people are turned off by that and *Google may punish you for keyword stuffing.* It's better to repeat yourself in a classy way where the keywords show up a few times on each page but not a dozen times.

Categories, Labels and Tags.

This is similar to keywords. Whenever boxes exist where you can enter categories, labels, tags, etc., think of them as keywords that will help identify you and the subjects of your website or business. Categories are typically more general while labels and tags are more specific. Keep these entries to single words or just a few words, not long-winded phrases. Also think of it as opportunities to mention your subjects and name that will assist search engines and others to identify you.

Links.

The more links connected to your blog and website, the better. Try to get your URL links on as many other sites as possible. Search engines record each time someone clicks a link that goes to one of your pages, and over time they start to recognize you're becoming more popular. Make it a habit to spread your links out to anywhere and everywhere possible, especially on all of the social media sites and places you visit as well as in the articles that you'll write (which we'll cover later in the Social Media and PR Public Relations chapters). As I'll discuss soon, *you can also leave comments on other people's blogs*, which is a great way to add input and leave your URL as most blogs that take comments will have a box for URLs. Leaving comments on blogs for subjects of interest is an excellent way to spread your URLs around.

Now, an obvious tip is to click on those links back to your blog and website. Number one, it's smart to make sure the links work, and secondly those clicks will register with the search engines.

Add your URL's directly to search engines.

Even though there are hundreds of search engines, if you simply focus on Google and Bing (now that Yahoo has merged search with Bing) you will be fine. In fact, you could probably only focus on Google and your SEO rankings could be terrific **over time**, but it still makes sense to do extras in this category.

There are several places where you can freely add your URL to their list. I've heard it said this is a good habit to do monthly, but that's not needed. Google even reports, *only the top-level page from a host is necessary; you do not need to submit each individual page. Our crawler, Googlebot, will be able to find the rest. Google updates its index on a regular basis, so updated or outdated link submissions are not necessary. Dead links will 'fade out' of our index on our next crawl when we update our entire index.* However, it will still take time for your URL to show up in a search with Google or any other engine even after you've submitted it correctly. It might take as little as a few days or as long as a few weeks. Unfortunately this is out of your control so be patient if it doesn't appear as soon as you'd prefer.

Here's the list of the best free places to add your URL for their directories:

https://www.google.com/webmasters/tools/submit-url - submit your sites directly to Google.

http://www.bing.com/toolbox/submit-site-url - submit your sites to Bing.

http://www.scrubtheweb.com/ - a great place to submit your sites to 10 search engines at once. This outfit also evaluates the effectiveness of your SEO strategies and provides recommendations such as "the Title should be less than 60 characters." Scrub The Web has been around since 1996 and has both free and paid services for helping anyone maximize her/his SEO performance.

http://www.webceo.com/ - this company claims to be the most complete SEO software package on the planet. It also has a free program to download containing in-depth website analysis and educational videos/literature. In fact, it has so much content and evaluations that it may be more than most people want to delve into. But the fact that this much assistance is free amazes me, and it certainly entices many customers to upgrade to their paid programs (although I think if anyone uses the free versions wisely along with the other advice I give here, she/he should be just fine).

Use the Google Webmaster Tools and Meta Tags or HTML Code to verify your sites.

Remember back when you may have created a blog with Wordpress, they should have provided these links to verify it with the search engines here - http://en.support.wordpress.com/webmaster-tools/. This procedure works for verifying with Google and Bing search engines by adding Meta Tags or HTML code that these search engines will crawl and identify. Help with this can also be found through the Dashboard of your Wordpress blog, *and this also works for any website.* If you scroll down the left side you'll eventually find a tab that says Tools. Click on it and scroll down to the Webmaster Verification Tools. There you will see the boxes that go hand in hand with the Meta

Tags you'll be asked to input by using the link above to visit search engines. And this will help too - http://en.support.wordpress.com/search-engines/.

For Wordpress.com and Yola.com I chose the Meta Tag Verification and followed their tutorials as these places make it very easy to insert. The Yola tutorial is here - https://www.yola.com/tutorials/article/Tutorial-Google-Webmaster-1285944435809/Promotion_SEO_Traffic_and_Advertising, and since Blogger is owned by Google that help is here - http://www.google.com/support/webmasters/.

With Webs.com, they only allow Meta Tags for Premium or paid members, so you'll use the HTML Code option. Here the Google Verification process is a tiny bit more involved but you can do it.

- Once you get to the Google Verification site - https://www.google.com/webmasters/tools/home?hl=en, click the Add a Site button and enter the URL of your website including the prefix as in www.example.webs.com.

- It will ask if you want to verify with a Meta Tag or an HTML file. For Webs.com I chose the HTML file, which it then created for me and asked me to Download the HTML file.

- When you download it, Open it then Save it by choosing Save Page As a Web Page HTML file on your desktop or in your folder.

- Then I returned to Webs.com where I Single File Uploaded it to my File Manager (Browse your Desktop or folder for that Google file and make sure the entire suffix looks exactly the same as the link Google shows).

- Then I went to Edit my Homepage, scrolled to the bottom and typed in "Google" (any letters will do). I clicked to highlight the word "Google," then went to Link to Insert a Link, from My Files and chose the Google HTML file and Insert.

- Then I published the page and returned to Site Manager.

- Once this was done, I returned to the Google Verify page, where it asked me to Confirm a successful upload by visiting a site it highlighted. (This should take you to a blank webpage with "Google" and many letters/numbers in the upper left corner. It should result in exactly the same thing if you click on your Home Page file link you just created over the word "Google." Test them in windows side by side to see if they're **exactly** the same; if they're not, try the process again.)

- Once I had visited the site in another window, I returned and clicked the Verify button and it worked instantly. I know this sounds complex, but if I can do it so can you.

Submit a Sitemap to Google.

With Yola and Wordpress, if you complete the verification process with Google, then Submitting a Sitemap is a simple extra step and something they recommend. Google says; *sitemaps are a way to tell Google about pages on your site we might not otherwise discover. In its simplest terms, a XML Sitemap—usually called Sitemap, with a capital S—is a list of the pages on your website. Creating and submitting a Sitemap helps make sure that Google knows about all the pages on your site, including URLs that may not be discoverable by Google's normal crawling process.*

This can be as easy as clicking on the Submit a Sitemap button and adding the suffix, /sitemap.xml to your Yola.com or Wordpress.com URL. Webs.com currently does not have the sitemap feature, but things may change so check back. However, you can easily verify each page individually if you want to be certain Google knows more than just your homepage. ***The HTML file is exactly the same for any page or any site that you create,*** so just load the HTML file onto a page and verify it with Google. Once you understand the process it takes very little time.

There are many other sites that submit your URL to search engines. Because some of them charge money and/or require your permission for mailing list opt-ins, they don't seem worthwhile to me. The above sites should be plenty, *but these things take time*, so be patient for results to show when you search for your website, name or keywords. Also make sure to get your links out wherever possible which we will discuss more in the next chapters.

Update your site on a regular basis.

Keeping your sites fresh with recent material will assist with new visitors and past members returning as well as getting the search engines to notice you. Search engines will check on your site as they regularly do, and they rank sites higher if they have recently updated information. For your blog this shouldn't be a problem, as you should add a new entry or update at least once a week in addition to posting comments from visitors. For your website, even a mere change of a new paragraph, video or link qualifies as an update. Do this once a month or so which will be plenty to keep the search engines noticing new information. If you feel the need to add more content but don't have the time to write it, you can add certain widgets that update themselves automatically. On Webs.com, for example, using an application for a Guestbook, Forum or Member's area will enable other people to add content that updates the site. It's like other people helping your search ranking.

Google Analytics.

This is similar to StatCounter but a lot more involved. It's yet another feature from Google that enables website owners to see much more detail about who is visiting from where, when, for how long and perhaps what they like and don't like about your website, http://www.google.com/analytics/. This is a tool you can use to better understand the whole process of generating traffic. For people who are serious about mastering their site's productivity, this can help to see what impacts their conversions from visitors to customers, contacts, subscribers, etc. There are tutorials and loads of information from Google for those interested. The free version is limited to 5 million page views per month for non-AdWords advertisers, but I'm guessing if anyone has that much traffic they'll probably feel okay about upgrading to some paid services.

The installation is the same for any HTML code widget, and Google says it often takes up to 24 hours to start seeing results. They can be installed within a page body or in a sidebar and they appear invisible.

Now it's time to Drive Traffic to Your Site.

The more visitors that go to your site, the better your SEO results will be. Having a regular flow and increase of traffic is beneficial for everything; it's not just for SEO help but for networking and doing business. I know what you're probably thinking: duh. Okay, it's obvious that driving traffic is the key to this whole thing, so how do you do it? The answer is anything and everything you can think of. I focus on free methods because I've found them to be equally as effective and infinitely cheaper as paid methods, but some people may decide to wisely spend money on this (as in advertising).

Our next chapters will discuss Social Media and Public Relations using multiple online methods, especially the free ones, to get your URL links out there and people coming to your site. That will directly assist the SEO results. Facebook, Twitter, Google Plus, forums associated with your subjects, press releases, blog posts, articles, etc., will all help tremendously in this regard. Even if you eventually decide to spend money on advertising, I highly recommend working all the free angles first.

(Update—since writing this book, I've written a guide on SEO alone called *Get On Google Front Page*. In it you'll find these tips and many more explained in thorough detail, much too involved to include in this one chapter. For those interested, that book is available at all major book retailers and this website, http://getongooglefrontpage.webs.com/.)

Social Media

I'd like to backtrack a bit to discuss social media and the concept of building an online platform. *Your online platform can be thought of as your internet presence,* and it's **vital** for successfully marketing a website and services or products at venues like Facebook, Twitter, Google Plus, YouTube, etc. Social media not only enables you to keep in touch with friends and family, *but it also enables multiple ways to connect with absolute strangers and for them to connect with you.* You must reach out to strangers from all over the world and enable portals for them to connect with you. When a perfect stranger contacts you from Botswana or Sri Lanka, it will probably make your day.

I'm going to list several sites I consider mandatory, but this category is truly *the more the better.* Keep in mind, just because you have 5 or more accounts on social media sites doesn't mean you have to be active there on a daily basis. Your presence, as in a profile and links to the website/blog, is all it takes. Of course, if you are active at some of these places it helps a lot, but it's not mandatory.

Here are several social media sites that are a must have:

Facebook.com.

This media mega-giant has well over 1 billion users, 50% of which log in every single day. That's amazing, 500 million users each day! The average user has 130 friends, is a member of 13 groups and spends nearly an hour a day on the site. 70% of users live outside the US, and Facebook is translated into 70 different languages. You can access it from mobile devices, and the people who do so are reportedly twice as active on the site. Needless to say, Facebook is the grand champion. *If you're not on Facebook, you should get on it right away. And if you are on it, you want to maximize your ability to make connections.*

So either start a Facebook account or make the most of the one you have. Upload photos and/or video of yourself. Make friends with as many people as you're comfortable doing. Comment on other people's photos and walls frequently which will leave a lasting image of your presence. Manage the settings to get the email notifications you want. (That's all handled through the Account Tab in your Account Settings under the Notifications list.)

You should also join multiple groups on Facebook that have to do with your subjects of interest. Groups are designated by the little icon of two heads next to each other. Just click on it and search for groups. When you find ones that you like, post messages on their group wall as long as the *content is open for public* and tell them about your websites when they're ready. You can even create your own groups. Make connections and be interesting because people prefer that.

(An important note here—whenever posting anywhere keep your messages interesting and fun without looking like a spammer. Try to add quality more than quantity. Keep posting regularly on the discussion boards, but alter them on each board so you don't get into trouble with Facebook. They have guidelines against spamming the exact same message in a cut and paste fashion to multiple boards and members.)

If you haven't done so already, creating a Facebook Profile Badge, Fan Page and Group Page or Page Badge are excellent ways to link Facebook users to your website and to have HTML widgets that link back to your Facebook pages. Return if needed to the chapter on Common Custom Modules/Widgets for details on this and for others that follow.

Twitter.com.

Some people have amazing results with Twitter although, for me, it's not as important as Facebook or Google Plus. Yet it's a must-have for social media. You need a Twitter account because there are exciting possibilities that exist on Twitter. You start "tweeting" regularly with things of interest and links to great articles, and people will find and follow you. It also helps to follow people who share things or deal with subjects that interest you, and these things can be "retweeted." What you'll learn on Twitter is you can write up to 140 characters and eventually connect with a lot of people. I'm not super active there, but I do have an application called Tweetdeck, which allows me to use this service even better. You can download Tweetdeck at http://www.tweetdeck.com/ or alternatives, which basically make Twitter a little easier to use and with more options.

How does someone use Twitter to create an audience and network? Keep it interesting. Share certain anecdotes or jokes or newsworthy stuff with links as you come across them. And yes, you can tweet about your website or blog but not constantly. That would get annoying to your followers, who might "unfollow" you.

The neat thing about Twitter is the fact that you might tweet a message others find interesting, and they might "retweet" (RT) it and so on until it gets seen by many thousands of people. I once did a blog entry on the uses for industrial hemp and made a tweet about it. One person who followed me "retweeted" it and the link to my blog site. Guess what? She had over 19,000 followers (a huge number back then), some of whom saw my tweet and visited my blog, which received far more visitors that day than usual.

These days many people have 50,000 or 100,000 followers or even more. I have far fewer but they're almost entirely writers and readers. You can either go for the big numbers or go for a relevant crowd to follow and follow back.

Use the @ **symbol** plus a person's Twitter name to include others in your tweets or make sure they get notified, especially in hopes of having them retweet.

You can also use *hash-tags* to help specify a message and gain relevant followers faster. Hash-tags are a way of searching within the billions of tweets for topic specific posts. It's simply the number symbol or pound sign (#) with a search term, like #SuperBowl or #Friday or even #elephant. To see if a search term is already being used, just type it in the Twitter search box at the top of the page and see how many results come up. Play around with closely related examples, like #fiction and #novel, to see which ones are more commonly used.

The same method can be used to find people with similar interests. Try hash tag terms for current events like this fictional example, #RenoFire. You can also play around with the terms in the Trends section on the home page.

There are many services designed to help increase your followers quickly. I don't use them since I prefer the organic method over time, but here are two:

http://www.tweetadder.com/

http://wefollow.com/

Here's a place to get a Twitter Badge - https://twitter.com/logo and there are many others like this one - http://www.twittericon.com/. Just choose a design, type your Twitter name in the box, and it will generate the code. Then copy and paste the html text code below the image you like, and when you insert it as a widget/gadget on your website or blog, it will become a cute birdie picture that people click to follow you.

http://www.twitter.com/

Google Plus.

This may be seen as Google + or Google +1 or simply G+.

In my opinion, *Google Plus takes the best aspects of Facebook, Twitter and LinkedIn while eliminating the worst.* (However, Facebook made broad scale changes to its platform as a result of G+, so don't be surprised to see all of the venues becoming more alike in time.) Presently, Google Plus has a design that can be your one-stop for all things social media. Like Facebook, you can stream wall posts of what's happening or share comments and include video, links, photos, chat, etc. Unlike the old Facebook, you can create different "circles" that these posts go out to (though Facebook has made changes to accommodate this ability; it's just time consuming to sort out for users who already have hundreds of FB friends). G+ circles can be composed of family, friends, colleagues, the bowling league, sexy lingerie club… whatever kind of circle you want to create. To me, this is a huge difference over the original Facebook as you can easily select what others do or don't see with updates and wall posts. As I said, FB made changes after Google Plus came out, but it's a hassle to change the status of friends when you have several hundred.

The G+ program will also recommend people to add and you can easily choose the circles to place them, which is a great way for them to discover you as well.

Like Twitter, anyone can add you to their circle to follow, and you can add anyone to yours. Unlike Twitter, you can identify who you want to see what, and you can do many things their platform doesn't support. Note that G+ also uses the **#hash-tag** for specifying subject matter and search ability.

The search bar at the top allows you to search Google Plus for people and content of interest. You can type in a name or things like recipes, books, dog-walkers in Los Angeles, etc.

Hangouts allow group video chat with multiple people, another very cool feature. These hangouts can also be made into YouTube videos with a click of the mouse, which can be perfect for doing interviews, tutorials or infomercials. I use them for a weekly show called Indie Authors. Here's an example of a G+ hangout I made that explains how to do this, http://www.youtube.com/watch?v=yYEnQAGTTec. You can use them for so many things, like having book club meetings with readers all over the world.

Because this social media site *does everything the other ones do and then some,* it feels like a must for independent authors.

There are plenty of tutorials on how to use Google Plus. Rather than trying to re-invent the wheel, here are some articles to check out.

http://www.readwriteweb.com/archives/how_to_start_ with_google_plus.php - article tutorial

http://www.stateofsearch.com/how-to-use-google-a-quick-guide-and-thoughts-on-google-plus/ - article tutorial

http://www.youtube.com/watch?v=5TDMObxEtEY&f eature=related - video tutorial

You can also find badges by searching the term, *Google Plus Badges*. Here's one place I found that creates a nice photo ID for a badge - http://turhan.me/+me/. (You'll need to add the URL hyperlink of your Google Plus personal profile page when you insert it on a website or blog.)

My personal strategy is reserving Google Plus for writing-business-networking, while I use Facebook for all my friends and family, although I also use FB for my group page. Group pages for businesses, products, artists or other categories can also be made at G+ by clicking the Create button in the Pages section currently listed in the More tab on the left side.

LinkedIn.

LinkedIn is the largest professional social networking site in the world. It's not just a place to put your resume, but there are other things going on at LinkedIn. With 135 million people from over 200 countries and territories, it's too large not to be a part of. At LinkedIn you can manage your public profile that's available for everyone to see, find and get introduced to people with connections in your specialty field and join groups very similar to Facebook. You can also be found for business opportunities, partners needed and join in discussions with likeminded individuals in private group settings. It's a smart social media site. Another bonus to being a LinkedIn member, as with Facebook, is that you'll be able to reconnect with old friends that you haven't spoken with in ages. That's a nice benefit as you're working on your online presence!

http://www.linkedin.com/

Other People's Blogs (OPB).

Other people write and update blogs constantly. These blogs are on every subject under the sun and usually have comment boxes where visitors can leave replies and continue the discussion. Not only do blogs get read by many visitors for years to come, but the comments get read as well. Comment boxes often ask for a URL to go along with your message. When your sites are ready, you'll always want to insert the URL address so that people who read the comment can click on the hyperlink.

It's mandatory to have something that adds to the discussion. Don't just spam messages about your website but add something helpful to the conversation or topic. Showing you can assist or entertain others will do much more to get people to click on your link. You can also type out the full URL address within the comment box that typically will become a clickable link.

Note that comments often require approval from the blog owner before they get published. But as long as it's something useful *blog owners usually approve comments because they want it to appear that many people read their blog*. Once the comment is posted it will act like a billboard for your site for years to come. One smart blog comment and link can literally attract hundreds of visitors to your site over time. Imagine what you can do by leaving comments on a few blogs every single day. Over the years that can add up to incredibly valuable free marketing. It's not an exaggeration to say that many thousands of clicks per year are attainable by simply making three smart blog comments per day.

So how to find all these blogs where you'd like to leave comments?

Google Alerts.

This is not a social media site but a social media tool. Google Alerts are incredibly helpful for anyone marketing online. I use them for my book titles, for my name and also for subjects of interest like self-publishing and ebooks. For those who aren't familiar with Google Alerts, this is how the company describes them; *Google Alerts are email updates of the latest relevant Google results (web, news, etc.) based on your choice of query or topic. Some handy uses of Google Alerts include:*

-monitoring a developing news story
-keeping current on a competitor or industry
-getting the latest on a celebrity or event
-keeping tabs on your favorite sports teams

I use them to help with marketing efforts and finding blogs of similar subject matter. For example, I get alerts each day about anything on the subject of making and selling ebooks. I can then click on those links and read the current articles and blogs. Usually there will be a comment box where I can leave a helpful comment and include a small blurb about my ebook and a link. As long as I'm not blatantly spamming an advertisement, it's really easy to get my message and links out there for others to click on. This helps generate traffic and rise in search engine rankings over time.

To get started, visit the site - http://www.google.com/alerts and fill out the form with your search terms and a return email. Once a day or so, Google will email you with any web content that appears. Then visit those articles and blog posts. If there's a comment box, leave a thoughtful reply and insert your URL which will be a clickable part of your name next to your comment.

Forums in General.

Whatever the subject of your website is about, it's a pretty sure bet there are forums dedicated to that somewhere. Find these forums and participate. For example, a simple Google search for "model airplane forums" or "model airplanes" should result in places to meet and great likeminded people.

You can also create forums within your website which is a brilliant way to network with others.

There are hundreds of other social media sites and tools. Because this field is growing exponentially, I'm only going to discuss and touch on a few of them.

YouTube.com.

You might not think of this at first as a place to promote your website but it's a great way to drive traffic, especially if you're fairly handy with video. A simple video about you and your site can be seen by hundreds to thousands of people in little time. Watch some YouTube videos on similar subjects to get a feel for what others are doing and decide if those ideas might work for you. Some people talk about their services and products for sale. Others discuss what they're about and how to find them. For my YouTube videos, I give examples of free advice on making websites and ebooks and include the URLs for those interested in learning more. The nice thing about these videos is the amount of views they get and the fact that some people relate better to video than to text ads.

Definitely consider possibilities with YouTube in terms of blurbs about your sites in ways that might gather some traffic. There are also badges for YouTube or you can create links to a profile page. You can also embed YouTube videos into a blog and website by copying and pasting the HTML code beneath the video. This is also smart for SEO rankings because the videos contain a large amount of data, and one factor Google considers important is the data size of your website.

http://www.youtube.com

Pinterest.com

Pinterest is all about sharing photos and images, typically within a theme, that others can also "repin," which is akin to retweeting for Twitter. Their mission is to connect people world-wide with similar interests and ideas. Pinterest should be considered by anyone with lots of imagery.

http://www.pinterest.com

Yahoo Answers.

Yahoo has an enormous forum under the title of Yahoo Answers. Both questions and answers exist from people all over the world for every subject imaginable. There are sections like environment, pets, health, sports, travel, business, arts, books, family, games, food/drink and much more.

You can browse the most recent questions or search for questions pertaining to your subjects. Then it's good to answer the question in a helpful manner. You can also leave a URL link within the answer box or the resource box. The good thing about Yahoo Answers is that they act as blog posts where people researching questions for months and years later can still stumble upon your answer, especially if it's chosen as the best answer and placed in the top of the results. Be sure to look for recent questions that are unresolved by tailoring the search to be for posts within the last seven days.

http://answers.yahoo.com/

Others to consider:

http://www.flickr.com/ - for sharing images.

http://www.digg.com/ - general social site and place to recommend blogs and sites.

http://www.metacafe.com/ - videos.

http://www.stumbleupon.com/ - discover cool stuff.

http://www.technorati.com/ - a collection of blogs and a great place to search for blogs of interest. You can also write articles for Technorati, something I've found to be very beneficial.

http://www.delicious.com/ - general social site.

http://www.klout.com/ - a place to connect all your links and measure online influence.

There are hundreds of others. One could write several books on this topic alone, so please understand if I haven't mentioned a social media site you enjoy. But even partially doing what I've recommended, these venues will be of tremendous value as you create links to your blog and websites. You don't have to be super active or try to do them all, nor would I recommend it, but make sure your URL links are in at least three of these and use Google Alerts.

Selling With PayPal

You need to read this chapter if you plan on selling products with PayPal or shopping carts. If you also plan on selling ebooks, then you really should see my book, *How to Make, Market and Sell Ebooks All for Free* at http://ebooksuccess4free.webs.com, because it gives many specifics on designing your website for that exact purpose as well as a myriad of other ways to sell ebooks.

For selling products from websites you have some options, but I'm going to discuss three: PayPal (PP), Ecwid shopping carts and Google Wallet (GW), which was previously Google Checkout. The later I'm barely touching on while a huge amount of time will be for PayPal.

Google Wallet.

At the time of this writing Google Wallet (GW) doesn't offer the flexibility or familiarity with customers as does PayPal (PP). Currently PayPal is the superior choice in many ways. I'm not going to discuss how to set up a Google Wallet account for these reasons:

GW only works with credit cards, while PP additionally works with bank accounts.

GW holds money, while PP's money transfer is fast.

GW interface for business is inferior to PP for things like sales records, transaction details, etc.

GW is not set up for international currencies like PP is.

GW has no live customer support, while PP does.

GW can't currently be used on eBay, should you eventually want to sell products there too. (eBay owns PayPal.)

Because we love Google for everything else and since things may change in time, we'll keep an eye on GW. If you really want to, go ahead and offer Google Wallet as a second payment option though I strongly encourage you to offer PayPal as well. While it may be true that a few potential customers would prefer GW because they're more familiar with it, there's no need to set up your website's store based on the exception and not the rule. Since I'm going to spend so much time discussing PayPal, I'll leave it at that. The Google Wallet set-up will be very much the same plus they have loads of tutorials if you want to learn more.

http://www.google.com/wallet/

PayPal.

Most of the world is familiar with PayPal. This e-commerce giant has revolutionized the way many of us shop. I remember the first time I used PayPal, feeling a bit nervous making a credit card transaction over the internet. *"Is this safe?"* I wondered. Well, those days are long gone. Now I buy almost everything directly online if possible, and more often than not PayPal is the method of completing the transactions.

PayPal accounts can be funded by a credit card or a bank account. As the recipient of a transfer you can request a check from PayPal, establish your own PayPal deposit account or request a direct transfer to your bank account. Any of these options are okay in my opinion.

PayPal fees are fairly low. PayPal takes about a 2.9% cut of any sale plus 30 cents per transaction. For example, if you sold a product for $10, you would make $9.41 after PayPal's cut. (Some may argue that a merchant account has a lower percentage of the cut, like around 2.3% with no transaction fee. However, merchant accounts have gateway and/or monthly fees, yearly fees and often sign up fees. If you do the real math you'll discover it probably takes $50,000 in yearly sales before a merchant account makes more sense than a free PayPal account. If you're doing that much business, you can always upgrade to a merchant account later.)

PayPal lets customers use major credit cards, e-checks or their own PayPal accounts to buy your goods. They make it easy to create Buy Now and Donate buttons that you can add to your sites very much like the HTML widgets from before. They'll provide reports of all transactions and basically become an online bank with no need for credit application, set-up fees, monthly minimums or any other hoops to jump through. They also pay quickly, transferring the funds from the customer to your account in little time. They claim to take security seriously, encrypting all information and preventing fraud.

That's not to say that fraud doesn't happen on PayPal. It's actually a constant discussion in the forums and a real bummer for many merchants. These people are usually selling tangible, physical products often to customers who receive the product and then claim that they didn't or the product wasn't as advertised. In many cases the dishonest customer gets to keep the product and have their money refunded.

How can you protect yourself from fraud on PayPal? Probably the most important thing is to make it absolutely clear what your goods are, explaining them in great detail and including multiple photos that give dimensions. Here are some important tips from PayPal:

Tips for Safer Selling. - https://www.PayPal.com/us/cgi-bin/webscr?cmd=xpt/Marketing_CommandDriven/security center/sell/TipsForSellers

1. Use overall precautions like **providing clear, detailed descriptions.** Buyers don't like surprises. Give a detailed description of your item and include photos or images where applicable. Images are especially important when selling in countries where buyers may not be as fluent with the language in which the seller wrote the listing. Let the customer know exactly what they can expect, how it's coming to them and what they should do in case anything goes wrong in the process.

2. Respond promptly to any inquiries and issues. Show buyers you are listening with a prompt and courteous response to all questions. Work patiently and courteously to resolve any issues, even with customers who are behaving badly. You never know who that customer might be, and if they have a sour experience with you they might go out of their way to write bad reviews and tell others to stay away from your site. Kindness just makes sense when dealing with customers on any level.

3. Chargebacks and reducing the likelihood of experiencing them - https://www.paypal.com/us/cgi-bin/webscr?cmd=xpt/Marketing/securitycenter/sell/Charge backGuide1. Chargebacks occur when buyers ask their credit card company to reverse a transaction that has already been approved. Common reasons for chargebacks include:

Item not received. Buyer pays for an item but never receives it.

Item significantly different than expected.

Unauthorized use. A buyer's credit card number is stolen and used fraudulently.

Hopefully issues like these will be the exception and not the rule.

Sign up with PayPal. You're going to need an account for buying and selling products which is a Premier account and is free. You simply need a valid email and a bank account or credit card.

There are two main ways to enable a PayPal payment on your sites: Buy Now or Donate Buttons and Shopping Carts. I'm going to discuss Buy Now buttons because that is all most people will need, and the set-up and implementation of a Shopping Cart is basically the same process. Even for those who have more than one product to sell, by simple creating two or more Buy Now buttons, all of their needs are met. Or if you have a plethora of products, the implementation for a shopping cart is very similar to that of a single button.

I'm about to give two descriptions of using PayPal Buy Now buttons; Method A is the built-in Web Store application on Webs.com and Yola.com, and Method B is manually creating and implementing PayPal buttons that will work on any page of any site (including those above). Method A, the built-in application, is simpler to do, but it's inferior in how the checkout is handled for digital goods like ebooks plus it's not ideal for multiple ebooks. Method A does work just fine for physical products that require shipping.

For setting up digital products to run on autopilot, as in a customer gets sent to a download page immediately after purchase, I recommend Method B, but I need to explain them both so you can decide. In case you really want the simplicity of the built-in Web Store for selling any type of product, I'll explain Method A first. If you have digital products (like ebooks or files) or if you want the checkout process streamlined, then Method B is the way to go.

Here's Method A: how PayPal works on the built-in Web Store application of Webs.com. (This is even easier at Yola.com which I'll explain below.)

- From the Webs.com Site Manager, you can click Add an Application where you'll see extra features that can be applied to certain pages of your site. If you click on the one that says Web Store and then Manage App, you'll be prompted to enter Products for sale. (This by default will be labeled the Products page, but you can change it to My Store or anything you want in the Site Manager with the Rename option.)

- There you can add the details of your product like the description, image, price etc. *Remember to be thorough in the Description box to avoid customer complaints later.* For the Product Image, that can either be uploaded directly from your computer or from your Webs.com File manager. Add the Price ($.01 if you want to test it first with a 2nd PayPal account and then change the price once you've confirmed it works). For physical products you'll need to comply with your state or country's laws on Tax, Options, Shipping or Status. These items can be edited later so no need to fuss about perfection now.

- Click Submit. You'll be directed back to the Products or Book Store page where you can see the new listing.

- Click on Settings. Check the PayPal box and fill in your associated Premier email for PayPal. Make it absolutely clear what you're selling in terms of what the product is: dimensions, descriptions, etc. Your Store Policies should explain what a customer can expect; *that after purchase customers will either receive an email confirming purchase and shipping information or a URL link to go and download their digital goods and how to contact you directly with an email should they have any problems.* Payment Instructions Field can be left blank or up to 40 characters explaining that credit cards or PayPal accounts work fine.

The Purchase Confirmation Message will be sent to customers after their purchase. Here you thank the customer and either instruct them on shipping information or direct digital good buyers to the URL address of the Download Page as well as insert a link so it is clickable. *For digital goods this is an aspect of Method A that's not ideal, because you need to rely on the customer clicking a link in the confirmation message instead of automatically being sent to the Download page.* Explain again how to contact you via email if anything goes wrong during shipping. For digital goods, also explain how to save the files and ask them please not to share the link with anyone else. (Note— don't worry too much about piracy of digital goods as the URL of the download page can always be changed later along with the PayPal confirmation message if you suspect illegal sharing.)

The Purchase Cancel Message is displayed to a customer that has an issue processing the order. Hopefully they haven't been charged, but if so PayPal will have information that you can check. In this box you should politely explain that you'll work as quickly as possible to settle any issues and leave your contact email so they can get in touch with you.

Unfortunately, only one confirmation message is designed to go out. *This is the other reason why Method A is not ideal for digital products, especially if you have more than one product to sell because you won't be able to send people to different download pages without giving them the link to both URLs in the one confirmation message.* You could rely on the honor system, but the real way to get around this (for those having more than one digital product) is to create separate PayPal buttons and separate corresponding Download pages which I'll explain next in Method B.

Here's Method B: how to set up PayPal buttons within a standard page on Webs.com, Yola.com or any other site like Wordpress, Blogger, etc. First we'll create PayPal Buttons before inserting them.

- After logging in to your Premier account at PayPal and clicking either on Merchant Services or on Buy Now buttons, you'll be redirected to Create PayPal Payment Button. Then follow these steps:
- Fill in the first box of Step 1 as a Product.
- Create a Buy Now Button box.
- Item Name is self-explanatory. For a digital product it can be your ebook title. If you're

offering more formats than .pdf, list them here as well.

- Item ID is optional.
- Enter the Price (you can input $.01 for testing with another PayPal account and make changes later).
- Customize Button (I don't recommend this because buyers are much more familiar with standard buttons. If you really want to customize a button with your own image, that's very similar to creating an HTML widget.)
- Shipping and Tax boxes need to apply to your state and country codes.
- Transactions Notifications can go to your email address.
- Step 2 is good to have Save button at PayPal checked. The Track Inventory and Profit/Loss boxes are optional depending on your quantities and interest level in tracking them.
- Step 3 Customize Advance Features is very important for digital products like ebooks! *This is how you can automatically direct people to a Download page after purchase.* Check Yes or No for customers changing order quantities depending on physical goods or digital goods respectively. Check Yes, for customers can add special instructions in a message to you. Check Yes or No (physical versus digital), for customer's shipping address. In the box that says, Take Customers to this URL when they cancel their checkout, check the box and input the URL

address of your website store so they can try again. *Here comes the really important part for digital products like ebooks;* in the box that says, Take Customers to this URL when they Finish Checkout, check the box and input the URL address of your Download page. Make absolutely sure you did that so people will automatically be sent directly to the Download page to get their digital product after purchase. Make sense? *That will make an ebook business run on autopilot.*

- Leave the Advanced Variables box unchecked unless you want to read the tutorial on what this can do.
- Click Create Button.

Next it will take you to a page that says, "You are viewing your button code." Here you can copy the HTML code for a Website, and you can also copy the URL address for Email. Both of these are important, and you should copy and paste each of these individually and put them in the "yourownfreewebsite" folder and save them as PayPal buttons (one for Website, the other for Email). The Website HTML code can be used for Webs.com, Yola.com, Blogger and many other hosts. *Both the Website HTML and the Email code is what you'll need for a Wordpress.com blog,* as Wordpress does not support code for web forms or Javascript. For this reason, both Webs.com and Wordpress will have slightly different methods of inserting buttons, which we'll cover now.

Insert your button on Webs.com, Yola.com, Blogger, or any other website (not Wordpress yet) that supports web forms and Javascript. This is very easy, just like the badges and other HTML codes we've inserted before. In most cases they can go either in the body of a page or on the sidebar as a gadget/widget or even both.

- In Webs.com, edit a standard page for the sale and place your cursor where you want the PayPal button, click the HTML icon at the far right of the toolbar (or you can find that widget the long way through AddOns-Tools-Other Stuff-Your Custom HTML), paste the Website HTML code and Insert.

- On Yola.com just drag an HTML widget within the page on the sidebar and insert the code. Your PayPal widget should be in place, though you won't see it until you Publish or View. Also add some text near the button to demonstrate that it's the Buy Now button to buy your product and for what price.

- If you also want it on the sidebar of a Webs.com site, place your cursor over the sidebar in edit mode, Click to Manage Sidebar, select Custom Module, Title it "buy this product for $(your price)" or something to your liking and paste the HTML code in the Body box, click Save, Save Your Changes, Done, View or Publish and Publish all Pages.

- You can also go back to Manage the Sidebar to select if you want the widget on the Home Page and/or the other pages and where you want them in order. (For some reason, I had to do this twice to get it right, but there they are. Two PayPal buttons showed up after a retry.)

- For Blogger and Yola.com, just add an HTML widget/gadget anywhere you want.

Follow up with action. It's smart to click on them, use a 2nd PayPal account and see if they work since you can't buy a product with the same account that sells it. This is also helpful to see the stats that PayPal provides on sales. You should have a functioning PayPal button.

I recently got a call from a writer using these methods, but she couldn't get PayPal to automatically send buyers to her download page after purchases. We went through every line of the form trying to figure out what was happening. Turns out some people have to make an adjustment to their Auto Return Settings. I did not, as many people are set to default with Auto Return Settings "on." In her case it was set to "off." If this seems to be a problem (getting PayPal to send buyers to your download page from the Step 3 Customize Advance Features tab), go to PayPal and Log In.

- Click on Profile.
- Click on Website Payment Preferences.
- Make Sure Auto Return is set to "on."

Even though I have multiple buttons, it has one button's return URL shown in the box. It doesn't seem to affect the other buttons, so not to worry if this isn't the URL you expect to see there. Check and make sure it works.

First I want to talk about Wordpress, and then we'll discuss changing your price from one penny to something else.

Now, let's talk about putting the same button into a Wordpress.com blog. Remember; Wordpress doesn't like forms or Javascript, so we have to use both the HTML and the Email code that you saved in Text documents in your folder.

- If you didn't save them, just return to PayPal, Merchant Services, My Saved Buttons, on that same button you just made click Action and View Code.

- Select and copy both the Website HTML and the Email tab and URL address (which you'll notice is a PayPal web address) and paste these codes individually into Text documents and put them in the "yourownfreewebsite" folder.

This link will help if you want to follow with pictures - http://en.support.wordpress.com/paypal/. (The Wordpress support tutorial uses a Donate button as their example, but it works the same with a Buy Now button.)

- Now go to Wordpress and log in to your Dashboard.

- Scroll down the left and on Pages click Add New and call it "Store" or something of your choosing. (If you want a choice of PayPal button images, you'll need to get another image's HTML code to display on your page. Get them here if you want - https://www.paypal.com/webapps/mpp/logo-center, and click Download to get the button's

HTML code, copy it and return to the Add New Wordpress page.)

- Switch from Visual to the HTML editor and paste the button's Website HTML code into the text body.

- Switch back to Visual and you should see the button there (if not retrace your steps and try again).

- Now it's time to add the Link for the Email code into the image. Highlight the button's image, click Link and paste the Email URL code (from PayPal) into the URL Link box. Select it to open in a new target window if you prefer. That should do it.

- Preview or Publish the page and check that it's working.

You can also add a PayPal button into a Wordpress Image Widget for your Sidebar.

- Drag an Image Widget into your Sidebar and Title it, "buy this product for $(your price)."

- The Email code for the PayPal button will go in the lower box that says, Link URL (when the image is clicked).

- You'll have to insert a URL address of a PayPal button's image into the upper box that says, Image URL. Note that this will be an image, *something that ends in .gif or .jpeg for example.* Find one with a search and try putting it in the Image URL box and the Email code in the Link URL box and see if that works. As I said before, if the size isn't right just alter the Image widget's Width and Height with smaller numbers until they're good.

(Note—Dreamweaver and Frontpage users or anyone experiencing issues may need to check the PayPal Integrating Tips link.)

Remember for digital products, to include the following instructions on your Download page: explain that they can save the ebook or file on their computer, where they can connect a USB or appropriate cable to download it to their e-reading device, and then they should use the safe-removal feature before unplugging their device. Also ask them please not to share the link with anyone else.

And that should do it. You can insert PayPal buttons on all of your sites, both on main pages and in sidebars. After testing, go back to PayPal and log in with your Premier account, Merchant Services, My Saved Buttons, Edit button and change prices from one penny to whatever you want and Save changes. This will automatically apply when someone clicks the button, as you can see in a test.

Hopefully soon, people will be buying your products directly from your sites, and the process will run smoothly and even on autopilot for digital products while you're sipping little umbrella drinks in Fiji (or perhaps sleeping at home).

http://www.paypal.com

Ecwid.

Ecwid is a shopping cart tool, which is an alternative to creating download pages and PayPal buttons. Some people will certainly prefer this method. I have to admit, many will find it simpler overall and less likely to need occasional checks against piracy. As with using PayPal buttons, there is *no installation required* for Ecwid, unlike most other shopping cart options. I still prefer making custom PayPal buttons, but that could be based on familiarity.

Ecwid has free and paid versions, though the free version should be fine for most people. If you want password protected download links for digital products, then that will require the paid version. Compare plans here - http://www.ecwid.com/pricing. Otherwise, the free plan works great.

Instead of creating a download page and directing a customer to it, Ecwid will host your digital files and include its link in the reply email after purchase. Otherwise, you'll need to arrange shipping for tangible products following purchases. After joining Ecwid for free, the process is basically this:

- Log in to your Control Panel.
- Choose Catalogue.
- Click New Product.
- Fill out the Name, Description, Price, and Upload an Image. Then Save.
- Click on Files if you have digital products, Upload your ebook in PDF (for example), enter Description. Then Save.

If you have multiple products, they can either be in the same category (*ebooks* for example) or a separate category for each product as my example below will demonstrate.

- I deleted all the sample products Ecwid provides (Fruits, etc.) to keep the clutter down.
- Go to Dashboard.

- Choose between the html codes for the Product Browser Widget and/or the Bag Widget (which is useful for people with multiple products) and/or the Categories Tabs Widget and/or the Categories Menu Widget. All of these can be used together or separately, depending on the look you prefer.

- Copy the Product Browser Widget Code and paste it in html box or mode on your site, probably a blank page that will become your store.

- Follow their video tutorial for inserting the html code to your website at their home page. Notice the html code contains Javascript, so it won't be compatible with free Wordpress.com blogs. You'll probably need to play around with it a bit as I did to get it to look right.

I've made an example of using an Ecwid store at one of my websites. Yours may look much different as you can customize the appearance. Here's my Ecwid example - http://your-own-free-website.webs.com/ecwidstore.htm.

They also have a forum and knowledge base to help with any questions.

http://www.ecwid.com/

As with most everything in this book, there are alternatives to free shopping carts. Here are some more:

osCommerce — requires installation. http://www.oscommerce.com/

Magento — requires installation. http://www.magentocommerce.com/

Zen Cart — requires installation. http://www.zen-cart.com/

There are plenty of other free shopping carts, but from what I've seen Ecwid is tough to beat. However, creating your own PayPal buttons is always a free and easy option too, one that I've had success with. If you're not sure which to choose, you can implement both to get an idea of which selling method works better.

Immediately respond to customers who bought your products from your sites.

This advice is so obvious it almost needs not to be mentioned, but *you should always respond directly to customers who just bought your products*. PayPal will send a confirmation notice of any sale that includes the customer's name and email address. I recommend emailing them as soon as possible; thank them for the purchase, remind them of the shipping details or download page's URL (in case something got messed up) and let them know you're available for comments/questions. You should also save their name and email addresses in a separate folder that designates them as buyers of your product. This way you can contact the entire group later if there's an important news flash, upgrade, etc. Of course, I do not recommend emailing frequently enough to be considered annoying, and always let them know they can unsubscribe to your mailings if they desire.

Developing and maintaining a relationship with your customers, even just a brief relationship, is extremely important to keep people genuinely interested in your happenings and for getting referrals from them to other potential buyers. And because most people try products that have been recommended to them, this little step will go a long way with generating more buyers from referrals.

Next we're going to cover extra methods to bring publicity to yourself, your sites and your products.

PR (Public Relations)

What do you do once everything's in place? That's the time to lean back and watch the traffic to your sites and orders start rolling in, right? Wrong. Marketing online is about patience, persistence and determination. These things take time; be prepared to put in extra devotion even after everything is in place.

The good news is that you're in the homestretch and just need some occasional persistence to keep the word out about your websites. Eventually, assuming people like what you're doing, a buzz will generate from others who will actually help you with the marketing by writing about your site and referring it to others.

Press releases.

Press releases are great ways to get the word out about you, links to your sites and your products. There are many companies that offer free press release services, and you can even submit a similar but slightly altered press release to a few different ones. The companies will each have more specifics on how to write and submit a professional press release. Some general things to consider are that these are not supposed to sound like promotions; they're meant to sound like news copy, what's happening and why it's interesting. Similar in rule to companies like Ezinearticles.com (see below), press releases should answer the questions of what, when, how and why this matters, and not be a big sales pitch.

Here are some companies that offer free versions of press releases:

PR.com

Free-press-release.com

1888pressrelease.com

PRlog.org

Write and Submit Articles.

If you can write the content within your webpages, you can write short articles. These can be articles about your sites and products/services, or they can be subjects that interest you. Like press releases, submitting articles is a great way to get your name and your URL links out there. Remember to be professional when writing articles and have them polished and of quality content. Then submit your articles to anywhere you can for free. You can even submit the exact same article to multiple places, maybe with minor alterations to each in the title and the first sentence or paragraph to help distinguish them. Here are some great places, and again more can be found with a Google search:

http://www.goarticles.com/ - the self-proclaimed largest free content article directory. I like them in that the articles post fairly quickly, usually within 48 hours, and they aren't too fussy with rules. They send a confirmation email once posted.

http://www.ezinearticles.com/ - expert authors sharing their articles. This site takes a bit longer and is much stricter on following all of their rules for accepting articles but is a great place once you get the hang of it. Your article must sound unbiased and not promotional whatsoever (the real problem with many of my own submissions). If your articles are denied, which happened to me plenty of times, don't worry. They'll explain exactly why and let you make alterations until approved.

Other Things You Can Do

There is a second way to create your website, by using a hosting company that doesn't provide site-building software. One can be built and designed entirely from scratch if you're a bit adventurous and computer savvy. There are literally dozens of free hosting sites that don't offer site-building programs. Instead they just offer the hosting while you create and provide all the website content. If manually creating a website from scratch is something you'd like to do, there is a free download for software called Kompozer. Kompozer is fairly easy to use (as far as web-designing software goes), making it ideal for non-technical computer users who want to create an attractive, professional-looking website without needing to know HTML or web coding. It employs WYSIWYG web page editing. It is user friendly but not nearly as easy as Yola.com or Webs.com site-building programs. I've used Kompozer and can vouch for its simplicity, but you'll need an instruction booklet or video to go along with it. Kompozer can be downloaded from http://www.kompozer.net/. There's also a great community support forum here - http://www.kompozer.net/community.php.

If you're going to try using Kompozer, then I recommend reading this free tutorial by Chris Farrell called *Create Your Own Website By 3:45 This Afternoon*. It's a great .pdf ebook that takes you step by step through building a website with Kompozer. I had to Google "free ebooks Chris Farrell" to find it, so you can too if this link isn't working in the future - http://www.free-ebooks.net/authors.php?author=Chris%20Farrell.

There are tons of companies that offer free hosting, so here's a brief list of web hosting companies that do not offer site-building tools:

http://www.50Webs.com/ - no forced ads, 5 GB/month bandwidth.

http://www.awardspace.com/ - no forced ads, 5 GB/month bandwidth.

http://www.leadhoster.com/ - top banner ads, 5 GB/month bandwidth.

http://www.host-ed.net/ - no forced ads, 10 GB/month bandwidth.

http://www.tekcities.com/ - no forced ads, 5 GB/month bandwidth.

Host or Guest an Internet Radio Show.

There are sites where you can create an internet radio show or be the guest on someone else's program. Hosts are always looking for new subjects to discuss and people to interview. If your subject matter and website contain information that would interest others, a radio show might be worth doing. You can be a guest or even create your own show, interviewing others with similar interests and subject matter. Currently, few shows have a lot of listeners and many shows have none, but that depends on their marketing as well as the interest level in the subject. Stats of listeners to any show can always change quickly. Here are two free internet radio sites:

BlogTalkRadio.com

TalkShoe.com

Free Auto Responder Email Forms.

Auto responders and subscribe forms are great ways to acquire emails of interested people. If someone visits your site and likes what they see, they're possibly going to want updates. Some sites have their own forms built in while others do not. Your form can be simple yet should describe exactly what they can expect along with a guarantee from you not to share their information with anyone. You should also include a way for them to get removed from the email list should they decide to do so. Email lists of happy customers can be an invaluable tool, especially if your site becomes popular and gets dozens or even hundreds of visitors interested in current happenings.

While the vast majority of Autoresponders are paid services, like Aweber, there are some for free that do the very most important part of the job, get email contacts for you. Here's a list of the few that I've found:

Responders.com - autoresponder and form for collecting information on your sites, comes with no ads. Request forms are easy to make with up to 10 questions that you can ask visitors. Easily integrates to a website with an HTML link. It doesn't create a contact list, though you can add emails of customers and those who express interest in an address folder. I also used this service. It seems to work pretty well. Unfortunately, it doesn't come with a safe unsubscribe link, so you'll have to add a line that explains how people simply email back with "unsubscribe" in the subject field or the body.

SendFree.com - autoresponder service with ads.

Maintenance

Back Up your Data.

There are some things to consider doing to keep your sites up to date and functioning safely. One thing is backing up your data and saving it on your computer and/or emailing it to yourself for storage. Fortunately Wordpress automatically backs up your content. From their support pages, http://en.support.wordpress.com/export/; *if your blog is hosted here at WordPress.com, we handle all necessary backups. If a very large meteor were to hit all the WordPress.com servers and destroy them beyond repair, all of your data would still be safe and we could have your blog online within a couple of days (after the meteor situation dies down, of course).*

But if you want to back up your blog content manually, you are free to do so by using the **Tools -> Export** *option described above (through your dashboard). This is still certainly a good idea, as if posts and pages are removed manually from an authorized user on your blog; there is no way to recover the posts. This will ONLY export your posts, pages, comments, categories and tags; uploads and images may need to be manually transferred to the new blog.*

For Blogger, click on Settings, Export Blog to backup all your posts and comments. To backup your Design/Template, go to Layout, EDIT HTML and click the Download link.

From Webs.com support; *we do not offer a way in which you can perform a "click button" backup of your site. However, we would never lose your files. The only manner in which your files are deleted is if you abandoned your site. In the event there is an issue caused by our servers we can always do a full restore.* Sounds like customer support can retrieve content although a user can't export files to their computer.

From Yola; *we certainly do multiple back ups of all our site data and we are in a position to restore all our customers sites simultaneously and quickly in the event of something unforeseen going wrong; but unfortunately we do not have a way to backup individual sites at this time.*

You can download your site in zipped format so that you have all of the files on your computer, although this cannot be uploaded back into the site builder, as this feature is in place for users who would like to download a site and upload it to another host. This might, however, give you peace of mind as you will at least have a copy of the site. To do this, click the down arrow of "Publish to the web" and click "Download Site."

Also, for testing purposes and to make sure you don't lose any data on your pages, if you are going to add any type of custom code to your page make sure to test it on a test site first; this will keep your page from breaking in the event that the code does not work properly.

One thing that's pretty easy to do for a site on Webs.com and Yola.com is to make a quick text document copy of each page. I just copy and paste the text from each page into a new text document, name it back up yourownfreewebsite.webs.com and save it in my "yourownfreewebsite" folder. That only takes a few minutes.

Just in case anything ever happens and I can't get my site restored properly, at least I won't have to retype all that text. The images and HTML widgets are pretty easy to upload again.

Review List of
Recommended Programs and Sites

YouTube.com - for tutorials on everything.

Facebook.com - best social media site.

Google Plus - other best social media site.

Twitter.com - unlimited potential for exposure.

Wordpress.com or Blogger.com - for blogs.

Webs.com or Yola.com - for websites.

StatCounter.com - for invisible hit counters, visitor data.

Widgipedia - your ultimate widget resource.

PayPal - online banker for your products.

PR.com - free press release company.

Goarticles.com - for submitting online articles and getting your link out.

Google Alerts - if anyone online is talking about your name, subjects of interest and for alerts on important blogs to visit and post comments.

GetResponse.com - free autoresponder.

Organizations to Donate to
Once You Can

Because many of these organizations are providing you, me and many others with free assistance, it's always smart to give back when you can. It doesn't have to be with money, but it can be with referrals and positive reviews. It can also be with money as I'm sure they'd appreciate it. Some of them have donation buttons and are even happy receiving a dollar for a cup of coffee. For the programs that I benefit the most from, it feels important to give back as I can. Hopefully it not only helps the company, but it helps other young authors or people in any field with their endeavors.

And so I encourage you to also give back when you can. It's good karma for everyone.

Cheating With Money

There may come a time where you'd like to spend money wisely to make some of these things better or add things that aren't available for free. I totally understand. With that in mind, as the epilogue to this book, I'd like to include a few things that I believe will make sense eventually to some.

Upgrading to a pure dot com without the extra suffix is a yearly charge of about $10 and will help with SEO.

Upgrading to ad-free hosting with more storage and bandwidth at many free venues is only about $3 to $5 a month in case your site develops substantial traffic.

Professional auto-responders like Aweber.com or GetResponse.com will be useful if your mailing list begins to grow beyond a comfort zone. They automatically update and manage your list which will be helpful if you have several dozen or hundreds on the email list.

AdWords and Pay Per Click advertising on Google. Google has a range of possibilities with advertising on any budget. You can spend small amounts or large ones and see if the results are worth it. Google also regularly sends coupons for amounts like $50 of free advertising that can be used to get started and see how it goes. You can always cancel before spending from your own pocket. The nice thing is that you only pay when the advertising works, when someone clicks the ad and either visits your site or buys a product. I still advise immersing yourself in all the free methods from this book first, but Google does have a nice program here - https://adwords.google.com/.

eBay.com

There are low monthly fees for selling products on eBay, and it can be a great option. I sell very few copies of my ebooks at eBay compared to my own sites or retailers like Amazon, but I do sell some.

http://www.ebay.com/

Using affiliate marketing companies to expand your sales force.

There are plenty of affiliate marketing companies like ClickBank that have small one-time fees to list products. It works on the free Yola.com sites but not for the free version at Webs.com (there you'd need to upgrade to remove the forced ad to allow the affiliate ad). Although it is my opinion that you must also be able to sell your products/services in the ways described here to have any chance at success with affiliate marketing.

The End

(Side note—if any customer of this book would also like a free pdf version that might be handier on her/his computer with all the hyperlinks, just let me know. You can also contact me to check for an updated version. I don't have any way of verifying who bought the book through a retailer other than if she/he left a review, so if that sounds fair just direct me to the review and receive a free pdf copy. Email jason@thelittleuniverse.com with *free pdf for my review* in the subject box. Even if you don't want the pdf, **it would be greatly appreciated if you would be so kind as to leave an honest review.**)

That's it for now. I sincerely hope you'll put these elements into practice and find your time and effort rewarded with successful sites and a satisfying online career.
Please keep in mind; online marketing typically is not a get-rich-quick scheme. It will take time. Search engines take months to really notice you. Being successful will require patience, persistence and perseverance to drive traffic in numbers that make you happy. I hope you'll remember this

whenever you're feeling frustrated by the process, as I have felt many, many times.

Thanks again for reading. I wish you the best of success. Contact me through the websites if you'd like or if you have further comments and questions.

Kind regards and best wishes,

-Jason

About the Author

Jason Matthews was born in North Carolina in 1967. He graduated from UNC-Chapel Hill with a degree in film and television. Jason lives in Pismo Beach, California, where he writes and teaches self-publishing.

He asks readers to **please leave reviews** at Amazon or anywhere you found the book.

He can be contacted through his websites, TheLittleUniverse.com - ebooksuccess4free.webs.com.

Facebook - facebook.com/Jason.M.Matthews

Google Plus - plus.google.com/+JasonMatthews/

Twitter - twitter.com/Jason_Matthews

Where applicable, it helps to include a personal note. Thank you.

Other Books by Jason Matthews

The following are available as ebooks and paperbacks at major retailers.

Better You, Better Me - there's a better version of you ready to be energized. The ideas in this book are easy to add to your life, and they work wonders.

The Little Universe - a novel about creating a universe and discovering incredible things within it.

Jim's Life - the sequel novel, about a teenage boy on trial who can see and heal the human light fields, being hailed a miracle healer as the world argues over his case.

How to Make, Market and Sell Ebooks All for Free – self publish on any budget and sell ebooks at major retailers, your own sites on autopilot and much more.

How to Make Your Own Free Website: And Your Free Blog Too - a how to book for building free websites/blogs and making the most with them.

Get On Google Front Page - dedicated to SEO tips, using Google better and rising in search engine rankings.

.

Please enjoy a sample of *Get On Google Front Page.*

Creating Quality Content

It's been said a million times because it's true. *Content is king.* The single most important thing anyone can do to help them rise in SER (search engine ranking) is to create and/or deliver quality content. In fact, a website could make absolutely no effort to enhance SEO factors and still be incredibly popular if it just has excellent content. Why? Because the visitors will still come, recommend the site to others, link to it, write articles about it, essentially do all the SEO work for it.

This often gets overlooked, but it's the foundation for online success. The more value a website has to users, the more traffic it gets, the more time visitors spend there, the more others will link to it, the more click-throughs happen, the lower the bounce rate (visitors leaving after seeing the landing page)... everything is made better by having good content on a website.

Google prides itself on developing a complex algorithm with over 200 variables that *attempts to match searchers with websites that have the content they're looking for.* This means Google really cares about user-friendly sites with high authority content delivering on the search terms they say they're delivering on.

This also means that Google does not like sites that are stuffed with keywords and provide little or no real value to the user. In fact, Google does not like such sites, and this gets into Black Hat SEO practices which we'll discuss in a moment. To make Google happy, you want to create websites with excellent content that make users happy, plus you can use the White Hat tips I'm about to share.

Google keeps space open for search results that have not been paid for. This is excellent news! Sponsored ads run on the side of the search results page. Sometimes a few paid ads also run at the top of the main body (shaded with a different background color), but the rest are free, organically produced search results. Again this means that anybody can get to page one and Google actually leaves room for them at the top.

First and foremost, your goal should be to provide a valuable user experience. And so here's the opening Get On Google Front Page Step to take:

GOGFP Step #1. Provide great content. Make your website the very best it can be so others will visit, spend time, share and link to it.

This is easier said than done. Obviously it's critical to optimize the items within your own control. The text must read well and be informative or entertaining. The images should be real eye-catchers. Video must be interesting and typically not too long. Everything that you provide must be at its very best. But what else can you do?

Here's a brief list of things you can add to a site to create more quality for any visitor:

- Link to existing articles on your subject. Find supplemental information and provide it as a helpful gesture. Places like EzineArticles are perfect for this and allow reuse with proper crediting.

- Add video whether it's yours or someone else's. Most people like having their videos shared as long as it's clear they are credited for it.

- Include interviews with authorities in the field or people of interest.

- Create a forum page encouraging questions and/or answers for anything related.

- Offer a Links page to other webmasters for mutual benefit, especially those that complement your work. It's like partnering with others who can help reciprocally.

- Include a database for further research.

- Add widgets that are informative or entertaining. The Blog Widgets is a good place for that. http://www.theblogwidgets.com/

Make an effort to provide visitors with as much value, information, entertainment, etc. so they will stay at your site, enjoy it, subscribe to it, recommend it and link to it. That alone will make your SEO life so much easier.

SEO (search engine optimization), what exactly is it again?

Simply defined, SEO is the act of assisting the search engines to find your website and thus improving the status of your ranking. Most people only look at the top page worth of results after typing a search term, and very few people scroll beyond the second or third page. So any search engine success is greatly affected by your ability to be on the first page and to stay there. Hence the need for smart SEO practices.

Google is well aware of this and spends much effort to educate users with literature and video on how to do this in ways that are both beneficial and done with integrity (or White Hat).

From Google's SEO Starter Guide;

Search engine optimization is often about making small modifications to parts of your website. When viewed individually, these changes might seem like incremental improvements, but when combined with other optimizations, they could have a noticeable impact on your site's user experience and performance in organic search results.

It's the job of search engines to find sites matching the criteria that people are looking for. Obviously it's best if search engines list your site as a place of interest for anyone using terms related to your subjects. To begin, you'll almost surely start out deep in their results, like on page 20, but over time you'll climb ever closer to the first page by adhering to the advice that follows. Eventually you will make it to page one.

Several years ago when I first created an internet presence and searched for my own name, I came up on page 17 and felt discouraged. In time I slowly climbed closer to page one even though my name is fairly common. There are approximately 600 people in the US with the name "Jason Matthews." Worldwide there are perhaps 800. Many of these people are referenced online, and in a "name branding" way we're all in competition with each other to be on the first page. Fortunately, my websites now experience decent search results for my name and, more importantly, for my subjects of interest. I will talk later about not only optimizing for your subjects but also branding yourself.

Although in a funny way, you don't need to worry about the search engines finding your website. They will find it; I guarantee that. To know immediately if they've found it or not, simply type in the entire URL into the search box as in http://example.com and see if it comes up at the top of the list. If it's not there, have no fear. It usually takes up to two weeks before they index a site. Give it some time and try again. I'll instruct how to submit your sites directly to Google and many other search engines, but even if you don't they will still find it. How do I know? Because Google Alerts is set up to notify me on subjects like my name, books, the download pages for my ebooks, etc., whenever anybody on Earth posts something on those items. It doesn't seem to matter how trivial or tiny the posting or the website is; like the concept of George Orwell's Big Brother, Google knows what's happening in Cyberworld.

However, you absolutely do want to maximize the recognition of search engines like Google and Bing *to not only find you but to associate the site with what you're trying to accomplish.* That means not only does Google see your site specializing in African coffee, for example, but that it believes you really know everything about African coffee because of the factors Google considers important. There are many ways to help in this regard, *but remember this takes time.* Search engine indexes also place value on visitor numbers, inbound links and how long a site has been in existence, and they prefer established sites with lots of data, incoming links and recorded visits over newer ones. Be patient and give it time as in weeks to months or sometimes even a year. As long as you stay diligent with the advice that follows, your sites will climb in the rankings slowly but surely.

GOGFP Step # 2. Be patient and treat SEO like a diet or exercise program. It takes time, and the results will be great if you remain persistent.

Remember; I'm about to share the central SEO tips, the same factors that got me to Google's first page in a short time. Please remember that these are basically shared in order of importance. *In general, the ones at the beginning are more important than the tips at the end.* That's been true for me so please put most of your emphasis on the beginning SEO tips, although they each are important and will vary depending on an individual's needs.

End of sample. The rest is available as ebook and paperback at major retailers.